Better Flies Faster

Better Flies Faster

501 Fly-Tying Tips for
All Skill Levels

David Klausmeyer

HEADWATER
BOOKS

STACKPOLE
BOOKS

Published by
STACKPOLE BOOKS
5067 Ritter Road
Mechanicsburg, PA 17055
www.stackpolebooks.com

Printed in the United States of America

First edition

Cover design by Caroline M. Stover.
Photographs by the author.

10 9 8 7 6 5 4

Library of Congress Cataloging-in-Publication Data
Klausmeyer, David, 1958–
    Better flies faster : 501 fly-tying tips for all skill levels / David
Klausmeyer. — 1st ed.
      p.   cm.
    ISBN-13: 978-0-8117-0744-2 (pbk.)
    ISBN-10: 0-8117-0744-X (pbk.)
    1. Fly tying. 2. Flies, Artificial. I. Title.
SH451.K5295   2011
799.12′4—dc22
                                  2010052887

Contents

Contributors

No how-to book is really a one-man show; every author stands on the shoulders of other craftsmen. This is a book about tying flies, so it might be more accurate to say I looked over the shoulders of others.

I could never have compiled all the tips in this book without the help and kind friendship of the following great tiers. Some of them contributed information specifically for this book; I swiped ideas from others when they weren't looking. Admittedly, creating this sort of list is unfair because it unwittingly omits dozens of talented men and women who have taught me many things about how to make better fish-catching flies. All of them have contributed to my evolution as a tier and angler.

Walt Ackerman
Don Avondolio
Dave Bargeron
Don Bastian
Al Beatty
A. K. Best
Marla Blair
Gary Borger
Jason Borger
Caleb Boyle
Dave Brandt
Herman Broers
Ian Cameron
Alan Caolo
Scott Cesari
Charlie Collins
Kevin Compton
Joe Cordeiro

Don Corey
Bruce Corwin
David Cowardin
Henry Cowen
Brent Dawson
Pat Dorsey
Roger Duckworth
Oliver Edwards
Capt. James Ellis
Phil Fischer
Frank Flowers
Steve Fournier
Jay "Fishy" Fullum
Keith Fulsher
John Gantner
Mike George
John Gierach
Rich Goodman

Mike Heck
Chris Helm
Anthony Hipps
Mike Hogue
Ken Iwamasa
Aaron Jasper
Claes Johansson
Capt. Doug Jowett
Bill Keough
Capt. Kent Klewein
T. L. Lauerman
Robert Lewis
Bill Logan
Ernie MacDonald
Zach Matthews
Kevin McKay
Mac McKeever
Bob Mead

Charles Meck
David Nelson, MD
Capt. Chris Newsome
Jay Nichols
Jack Pangburn
Ted Patlen
Bob Popovics
Dennis Potter
Andrew Puls
Al Quattrocchi

Ed Quigley
Al Ritt
Paul Rossman
Scott Sanchez
Eric Schmuecker
Tom Schmuecker
Peter Smith
Capt. Ray Stachelek
Shane Stalcup
Harrison Steeves

Michael L. Stewart
Rick Takahashi
Dick Talleur
Steve Thornton
Hans van Klinken
Seth Vernon
Dr. Tom Whiting
Vince Wilcox
Leslie Wrixon

CHAPTER 1

Getting Started

The First Rule of Fly Tying

When talking to clubs or leading classes, I always start by asking this question: What is the first rule of tying flies? The answer is so obvious no one ever gets it. The first rule for tying nice flies is to wash your hands! This is especially true when using light-colored threads, flosses, and similar materials. Even the oils from your hands can discolor these ingredients and spoil the appearance of your finished flies.

Organize Your Favorite Patterns

The Internet is a great source of new patterns; the problem is remembering all the wonderful flies you discover. When you find a pattern you like, simply print it out and place it in a binder. Each page will have one pattern, so there is ample room to make notes and jot down ideas. If you're good with computers, you can even copy the pattern from whatever website you're using, paste it into your word-processing program, and format the text to your liking. This way all of the patterns will look somewhat alike, and your archive will be a little more enjoyable to use.

Here's a collection of three trout flies that will catch fish almost anywhere in the world (clockwise from left): Stimulator, Elk-Hair Caddis, Poxyback Stonefly. Hone your skills on a limited number of flies, and add new patterns and tying materials gradually.

"What Should I Tie?"

That's the first question every fledgling fly tier asks. There are literally thousands of patterns, so it's easy for new tiers to get lost. Here's a simple solution: Ask the fellow at your local fly shop to name the top three to five flies that catch fish in your area. He's probably a pretty good fisherman, and he talks with a lot of anglers and sees what they're buying.

Concentrate on tying those patterns to build your confidence; nothing builds self-assurance like catching fish with your own flies. This is also a great way to keep costs down while learning the basics; there's a good chance you'll be able to use some of the same materials to tie more than one pattern.

Check out this flotilla of Dave's Hoppers, one of the most popular grasshopper imitations. I probably won't run out of hoppers even after a couple days of hard fishing. In addition to having ample flies, tying batches of the same pattern is the best way to learn how to tie a fly.

Better by the Dozen

Tie *at least* a dozen of any pattern at one sitting—preferably two dozen—if you really want to learn a pattern. After two dozen flies, you'll begin to understand the intricacies of the fly and they will all start to look the same. "This, of course, doesn't apply to the Humpy," says fly-tying authority Harrison Steeves. "It takes about one thousand of these to get it right."

Do the Best You Can

Strive for perfection on all your flies. Placing a poorly tied fly in your vest is not the way to become a better fly tier. If you tie a disproportioned fly, cut the materials off the hook with a razor blade and start over.

Hybrid Flies

There are many tried-and-true patterns, but you can have a lot of fun combining flies. Experiment and combine pieces of your favorite flies to create a new pattern. The famous Half-and-Half was created by combining Lefty's Deceiver and the Clouser Minnow.

To Fix a Fly— Or Not?

If you make a mistake when constructing a fly, it is often much more expedient to strip the materials off the hook and start over rather than trying to repair the damage. You really will end up with a better fly and save time. It all depends on how serious the mistake is, but sometimes it's just easier and faster to start over.

Make Half Hitches Between Steps

The half hitch is one of the most useful knots in fly tying. Make one of these simple knots after tying each new material on the hook. A half hitch adds very little bulk to the fly, and it will prevent the fly from coming apart if you break the thread or accidentally lift the bobbin.

Walk Before You Run

Don't rush your tying. Tying too fast results in mistakes and poorly tied flies. Work at a comfortable pace to tie better flies. Increased speed will come with experience.

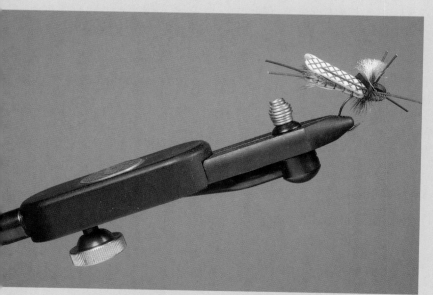

Here's the Regal vise in action. The head easily tilts up and down, and from side to side.

A Vise With an Adjustable Head

It's all a matter of preference, but I like either a rotary vise or a vise with an adjustable head. A rotary vise allows me to easily turn the fly over and see the pattern at different angles. (In this book's tying steps, I use a rotary vise manufactured by Renzetti.) A vise with a head that adjusts to different angles, however, is also convenient because you can tilt the jaws to gain access to different parts of the hook while tying, or to look at different parts of the fly.

Which Tools Do You Really Need?

Don't get overwhelmed by all the tying tools you see in your local fly shop. In addition to a vise, you need only a few tools to get started and tie hundreds of different patterns. And, if you purchase high-quality tools, you'll have them the rest of your life. Add more tools only as needs arise and you gain experience. One more piece of advice: don't be afraid to ask for a demonstration of any of the tools you are considering purchasing, especially the vise.

From left to right the essential tools are

- Hair stacker
- Bodkin
- Bobbin
- Scissors with medium serrations
- Hackle pliers

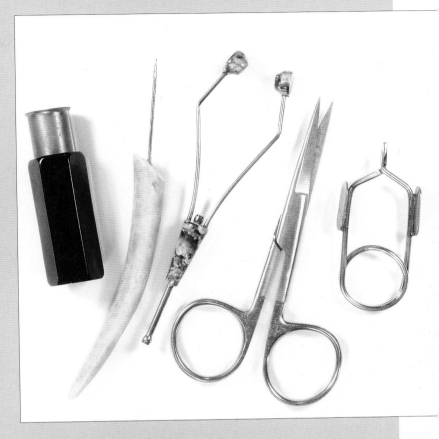

Study Streamside Entomology

It's surprising how many tiers make flies following only the photos of the insects and other forms of trout food they see in books and magazines. To really excel at fly tying, be sure to read a good book about aquatic entomology; many have been written geared toward fly tiers. Many fly shops also offer classes on aquatic entomology.

Start Big

If you are tying several sizes of the same pattern, start with the larger size and progress down in size. For example, tie six size 14 Pheasant-Tail Nymphs, and then tackle the size 18 flies. Hone your skills on the larger fly, and then tie the smaller version.

Just a Pinch Will Do

The pinch wrap prevents the thread from twisting wings around a hook shank. Tie the tail and body of the fly, and prepare the wings. Now you're ready to tie the wings in place using the pinch wrap. This technique works for tying the wings on both wet and dry flies.

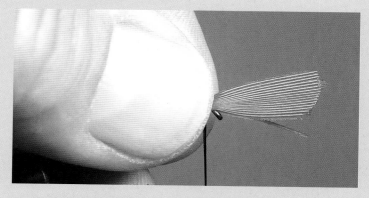

1 Pinch the wings to the top of the hook using the thumb and forefinger of your free hand. Raise the thread straight above the hook. Slip the thread between your thumb and the nearside of the hook. Loop the thread over the top of the wings. Next, slip the thread between your index finger and the backside of the hook.

2 Pull the bobbin straight down to tighten the loop and secure the wings to the hook. Add another pinch wrap. Now you can examine the wings. If everything looks good, you may finish the fly; if the fly does not look right, unwrap the thread, remove the wings, and try again.

3 Here's my completed wet fly. The wings are positioned directly on top of the hook.

Two are Better than One

When completing the fly, use two whip-finishes. The second knot assures that the fly will not come apart when fishing.

Use Quality Materials

Select the best materials and hooks you can afford. It is easier to tie flies using high-quality materials, and your finished flies will be better. In the long run, you might even find that it is less expensive—and certainly less frustrating—than struggling with inferior goods.

Three Attributes of a Good Fly

A good fly mimics the size, shape, and color of real trout food. Designing a fly with these three attributes almost guarantees success.

Drops of Cement Increase Fly Durability

Use your bodkin to place tiny drops of cement on the fly after each major tying operation. For example, place a drop on the thread wraps holding the tail. Place another drop on the wraps that finish off the body, and put another drop at the base of the wings. Adding these small drops takes little time, and they will increase a fly's durability.

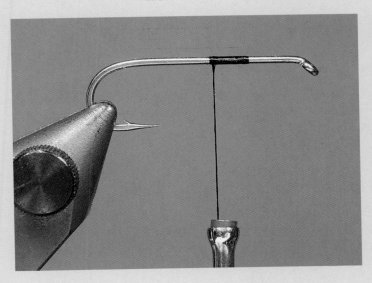

Short Working Thread

Whenever possible, tie with only an inch or two of thread extending from the end of the bobbin. Working with a short amount of thread will allow you to maintain better control and accuracy.

The tip of the bobbin is only an inch from the hook. I'll be able to easily control the thread and make exact wraps.

Impressionistic Flies Often Work Best

Some of the simplest patterns are also the most effective. Rather than dressing up, try dressing down—or simplifying—some of your favorite flies. Concentrate on recreating the features that establish the outlines of common forms of trout food. You might be surprised how well they work.

The classic Hornberg is a good example of an impressionistic fly. About a week before writing this chapter, my wife and I spent several afternoons using Hornbergs to catch brook trout that were freely rising to adult damselflies. This pattern made enough lifelike impressions on the water that the fish went wild for it.

Sparse Flies

Most new tiers use entirely too much material on their flies. Sparsely tied flies, however, are easier to cast and often create better impressions of the living organisms that you are trying to imitate. When in doubt, reduce the amount of material you are using by half, and you will rarely go wrong.

Test Your Flies Before Fishing

Developing a new pattern? Tie it to the end of a piece of monofilament, and swim the fly through a fish tank or even your bathtub. This simple test will give you the opportunity to see how the fly looks in the water from all angles. While it is important that a fly looks good in the vise, what really matters is how it looks and performs in the water. If you're not entirely satisfied with the look, feel, or action of the fly, you can make adjustments.

Change Your View

To make sure materials are positioned properly on the hook, view the fly from different angles. Look straight down the shank to see that the materials have not rotated out of position; this is sometimes difficult to see when examining the fly from the side. This is one of the big advantages of a rotary vise: you can easily turn the fly to examine it from all angles.

Here I'm turning a waking fly in a rotary vise.

The Crystal Bugger is a good trout fly, and it is an especially effective pattern for catching bass. When tying the Crystal Bugger and similar flies, brush the hackle fibers back while you work to prevent binding down the fibers.

Neater Spiral-Wrapped Flies

Every beginning fly tier learns to make the Woolly Bugger; the chances are this is the first pattern you make in your fly-tying class. The chances are just as great that you will continue making this fly throughout the rest of your fly-tying career; it's just that good of a fishing fly. When spiral-wrapping the hackle on a Woolly Bugger, Woolly Worm, and similar flies, brush the feather fibers back after each wrap. Taking care not to bind down the fibers yields a bushier fly that has lots of fish-enticing action.

Learn Thread Control— Lesson #1

Thread control is the most important fly-tying skill. The first step is to determine the breaking strength of the thread before you start tying materials on the hook. Wrap the thread on the bare hook. Next, pull the bobbin until the thread snaps. Repeat this a couple of times until you get a feel for the strength of the thread. Repeat this procedure every time you switch to a different size or brand of thread. (*Note:* The heaviest threads, Kevlar, and gel-spun will probably bend the hook before snapping.)

Learn Thread Control— Lesson #2

Once you feel comfortable with wrapping thread, experiment with tying various materials to the hook. Observe how they react to the pressure of the thread. Do they push away and refuse to be trapped? Do they flare, turn, or flatten, or does the thread cut through the material? Try wrapping the thread at angles, and use different amounts of pressure. Spend an evening repeating these experiments, and proper thread control will quickly become second nature.

Mastering Thread Torque

Think of thread torque as thread friction. For example, when you tie a dry fly such as an Adams, does the wing on the far side of the hook always wander off like it has a mind of its own? That's the result of thread torque. As you wrap the thread over the top of the hook, the thread grabs the material and locks it down, but as you wrap down the far side of the hook, the thread grabs the material on that side and rolls it out of position.

When tying the venerable Adams or a featherwing streamer such as the Gray Ghost, pull up—not down—to lock the material to the far side of the hook. Make a second pinch wrap under the fly, and secure the materials by pulling up and back, not down. It is remarkable how well this works to tie materials in the proper position.

Exaggerate Attractor Patterns

Attractor patterns are great for catching striped bass, tarpon, smallmouth bass, and many other species. Try adding a little extra material to exaggerate certain aspects of these flies. Tie on extra Krystal Flash, Flashabou, Sili Legs, and tailing feathers. You can always trim these materials back when fishing if you find them a bit over-done, but sometimes these overdressed patterns really fire up the fish!

Batch Tying

When tying a large number of flies, making the flies in stages sometimes speeds the process. For instance, when making a group of bead-head nymphs, slip beads on all the hooks before tying. Next, tie the tails and abdomens of all the flies. Finally, make the thoraxes and wing cases. Use a couple of half hitches or hand-tied whip-finishes between stages to prevent the flies from coming apart. Step-by-step tying will keep your workbench cleaner and better organized, and you'll proba-bly discover that by concen-trating on individual parts of the patterns, the quality of your flies improves.

Spin Flat Thread Clockwise to Increase Its Strength

Flat fly-tying thread is made with many ultra-fine, unbound strands. Spin the bobbin clockwise to wind the thread tight like rope. This increases the strength of the thread.

I've spun this flat thread clockwise, like a narrow rope. Notice the thin, strong wraps.

Remove Twist from Flat Thread

With each wrap of thread you make around the hook, you will make one twist in the thread. If you want the thread to lie flat, such as when making a level under-body or a fine floss body, spin the bobbin counter-clockwise to remove the twist and keep the material lying flat on the hook.

Here I've spun the spool counterclockwise. You can see the broad, flat, smooth thread wraps.

Here's my rendition of a Copper John tied on a size 14 wet-fly hook. Tie the Copper John in a variety of sizes and colors to match almost any small- or medium-sized mayfly or stonefly nymph.

The Bestselling Fly

Umpqua Feather Merchants is the world's largest manufacturer of commercially tied flies. According to Bruce Olsen, the sales manager of Umpqua Feather Merchants, the Copper John is the best-selling trout fly in the world. "We sell them by the tens of thousands," Bruce says, "and that's just the original copper-colored version. When you add in all the color variations of that pattern, the numbers get to be absolutely staggering."

Thousands of anglers can't be wrong. If you haven't tied and fished with the Copper John, it's probably time you did!

In Your Mind's Eye

Before tying a new pattern, visualize the finished fly first. Place the hook in the vise and determine the proportions of the tail, the body, and the other parts. If you're developing a new pattern, sketch it out before tying it. Plan ahead and you really will have greater success.

A Fly's Castability

Yes, the goal is to tie a fly that catches fish, but before you can catch a fish, you have to cast the fly. It's surprising how many flies are almost impossible to cast. Some dry flies have stiff wings that cause these patterns to twirl like propellers and twist and tangle fine leaders. The tails and wings on some streamers easily foul around the hooks and spoil the appearance of these flies in the water. And far too many tiers sock lead wire and extra-large dumbbell eyes to their flies to make them sink quickly; these small bricks are dangerous to cast, and a better and safer approach is to fish moderately weighted patterns with a fast-sinking line.

When designing a new fly, or tying one from a recipe you discover in a book or online, first determine whether you will be able to cast it with your choice of tackle, or be prepared to match the tackle with the flies being cast. Don't expect to cast a Clouser effectively with a 3- or 4-weight rod.

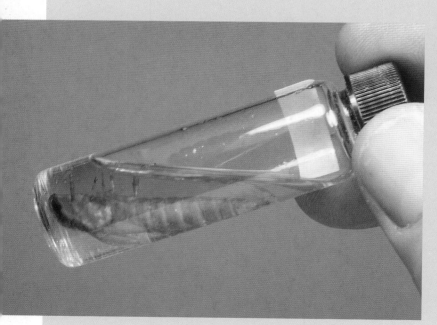

Collect a Few Insects During Your Next Fishing Trip

Vials filled with rubbing alcohol are excellent for storing insects collected from your favorite streams or rivers. Note the insects' colors and the proportions of their bodies. Even if you tie only simple patterns such as the Hare's-Ear Nymph and Czech Nymph, strive to match the general length and width of your sample nymphs and larvae.

Collecting insects is fun and educational. It will make you a better angler and a better tier.

Good Dry-Fly Capes

Acquiring good feathers for tying dry flies is one of the most expensive purchases you will make. You may wish to buy an entire cape of feathers. The cape is the pelt of feathers acquired from the neck area of a male chicken. What are the attributes of a quality cape? First, a good cape has a wide variety of sizes of feathers so that you can tie flies in a range of sizes. The individual feathers have strong quills that do not break or split when wrapped around a hook. Each feather has a large count of individual fibers of relative equal length. And finally, the base of each feather will have few fluffy—and generally useless—fibers.

Select capes in colors to tie the flies that catch fish on your local waters; brown, grizzly, light tan, and gray (often referred to as "dun") are usually the most important. To save money, don't be afraid to substitute colors of feathers when tying a fly. For example, I can't think of a pattern that calls for a dun hackle that you cannot tie with equal success using a grizzly feather, and tan is usually a perfectly acceptable substitute for brown.

This grizzly dry-fly cape, which was dyed olive, has hundreds of fine hackles. This specific cape was produced by Keough Hackle.

Variant Capes are a Bargain

One of the attributes of a grade 1 cape is that its feathers are a uniform color. The hackles on a brown cape will all be an equal shade of brown. Remember, however, that hackles are a natural product, and very little in nature has a single uniform color. As a result, a large number of capes have at least a few feathers that do not match the overall color of the neck. These capes are called "variants," and although the feathers may be excellent for tying flies, they are downgraded and less expensive. Closely examine the hackles on a grade 2 cape; it's very possible that they are ideal for tying flies, but the neck has the lesser grade only because it contains a few off-color feathers.

Do you see the few brown feathers on this grizzly Cree cape? Most customers in your local fly shop would pass this neck up and select another, and as a result, most hackle growers would downgrade it. That's too bad, because the hackles on this variant cape are ideal for tying flies. What's the lesson? Carefully examine those grade 2 and grade 3 necks; their lower grades may have nothing to do with the quality of the individual feathers for tying flies.

Learn Not to Crowd the Hook Eye

Start the thread at the front of the hook a distance equal to the width of one hook eye. When tying the fly, do not tie materials in the bare space behind the hook eye; reserve this area for wrapping the thread head and making the whip-finish knot. This visual reminder will eliminate the common frustration of running out of room to make the head and tie off the thread.

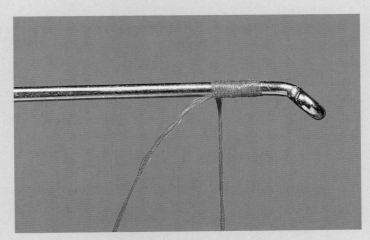

Start the thread on the shank a distance equal to the width of the hook eye. Save this bare space to make the head of the fly.

Simple Flies for Fishing Deep

The most successful anglers say you have to be daring when you fish; in other words, you can't worry about losing a few flies. Simple nymphs are best for fishing deep near the streambed. You'll occasionally snag the streambed and will lose flies. Use nymphs that are easy to tie and require only a few materials, and fish fearlessly.

Start With a Good Thread Base

It is difficult to tie many materials to a bare hook. For example, when trying to tie on wings or a tail, there's a tendency for the material to slip around the hook shank and not stay in place. This problem is especially true when tying hair wings. Always start by wrapping a good thread base. The thread creates friction on the hook, and the materials are less likely to slip around the hook.

Secure Thread Base With a Drop of Cement

To keep a fly from twisting on the hook, place a drop of cement on the shank before starting and wrapping a thread base. The glue locks the thread to the hook and makes a secure base for the following materials.

Checking Your Progress

When tying a pattern for the first time, it's a great idea to keep the flies on a magnetic board in front of you. Check for consistency and determine where you'd like to make changes and improvements. And since they are resting on a magnetic board, it's easy to remove a fly for closer examination. Having the flies lined up in front of you is the best way to gauge your progress.

Select More, Then Use Less

John Gierach is probably the best-selling fly-fishing author. He has written several beloved books, including *Trout Bum*. Before that, John was a professional fly tier, and he was one of the first authors who contributed to *Fly Tyer* magazine in the 1970s. John doesn't just write nice fishing stories. When it comes to fly fishing, he's the real deal.

John turned me on to this tip for tying hair tails and wings on flies. When clipping the material from the tail or hide—such as calftail or elk hair—select a slightly larger bunch than you will actually use. You can then pull out a few hairs until the bunch is the correct size. As John correctly points out, it's much easier to discard a few hairs than to add more.

A Spiral-Wrapped Thread Base

It is common practice to wrap a layer of thread on the hook shank before building a fly; the goal is to create a surface that locks the materials in place. In the old days this worked with wax-impregnated threads, but today's synthetic threads are slippery and much smaller in diameter; covering the hook shank may waste valuable time and produce a slick surface. Spiral-wrapping the thread—leaving small gaps between the wraps—creates a surface that prevents the materials from slipping down the hook.

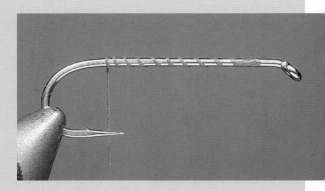

Spiral-wrapping the thread on the hook creates ridges that prevent materials from slipping down the hook shank.

Dry-Fly and Hen Hackle

Dry-fly hackle comes from male chickens, and just as the name implies, you use it to tie high-floating dry flies. But what do we do with hen hackle?

The hackles from hen chickens are softer and best used for wrapping the collars on wet flies or making the tails and wings on some streamers. The soft fibers move in the water and imitate the struggling of drifting nymphs or the swimming action of baitfish. Hen hackle comes in the same range of colors as dry-fly feathers. Be sure to carefully examine the grade 2 hen capes in your local fly shop; they are often variant pelts containing only a few off-color feathers, but the hackles themselves are ideal for tying flies.

Here we see a coq de Leon hen cape. Whiting Farms, one of the world's leaders in producing fine fly-tying hackle, offers coq de Leon. The soft, mottled feathers on these necks are a brilliant choice for tying wet flies and the tails and legs on nymphs.

Tying in the Vertical Plane

It's generally easier to wrap thread straight up and down—vertically—in relation to your tying bench. Sometimes this is a challenge, especially when using a curved-shank scud hook. There's nothing wrong with repositioning the hook while you work so that you are always wrapping in a vertical position. Either tilt the head of the vise up or down to keep the thread in the vertical plane, or reposition the hook in the vise jaws. Remain comfortable while tying, and you will produce quality, fish-catching flies.

1 Place the hook with the point facing down at about a 45-degree angle. Start the thread and wrap the first half of the body. Spin dubbing on the thread, and start wrapping the body. Notice that the thread remains pretty much in the vertical plane.

2 Reposition the hook to the upright position and continue wrapping the dubbing. Throughout this procedure, I have been wrapping the thread in a comfortable, vertical position.

How Many Feathers Are On a Dry-Fly Cape?

Fly-tying authority A. K. Best counted the individual feathers on a group of Tyers Grade dry-fly capes provided by Keough Hackle. Bill Keough is a leading grower of poultry that yields some of the finest feathers in the world for tying flies. (At the time of this writing, the suggested retail price of Keough Tyers Grade capes is $49.95 apiece.) All of the necks A. K. examined contained large numbers of feathers for tying everything from size 10 to size 28 dry flies, and some capes had hackles suitable for making size 30 flies. (If you can find hooks that small!) A. K. gave the following count of individual hackles, and noted that many feathers were actually long enough to tie more than one fly.

Medium dun: 793 hackles, which is enough to tie 66 dozen single-hackle flies
Brown: 909 hackles, which is enough to tie 75 dozen single-hackle flies
Grizzly: 886 hackles, which is enough to tie 73 dozen single-hackle flies
Black: 684 hackles, which is enough to tie 57 dozen single-hackle flies

A. K. Best counted 886 useable hackles on a grizzly cape. For the average tier, that's a lifetime supply of dry-fly feathers.

What is a Saddle Hackle?

Saddle hackle comes from the back—or saddle area—of the chicken. These long feathers are traditionally used to tie the wings on streamers, but many hackle farmers now offer great saddle feathers that are ideal for tying dry flies. You can use one of these long, fine feathers to tie three or even four flies. The Whiting 100 packs, which you will find in many fly shops, contain enough saddle dry-fly feathers to tie approximately one hundred flies and are a terrific value for your money.

Bright Indicators on Dry Flies

A bit of brightly colored closed-cell foam or poly- propylene yarn, tied to the top of a fly, is a terrific way to track the pattern on the water, especially under poor light conditions. I've never met an angler who claimed that the indicator spooked trout; the fish seem far more interested in the footprint the fly makes on the surface than the colored indicator above. And, in many cases, the fish can't even see it—the indica- tor material is tied over another material.

Vince Wilcox is one of my favorite fly designers. He often adds a sprig of bright polypropylene yarn or foam to a dry fly so he can track the pattern on the water. This is one of Vince's great flies.

Substituting Materials

Don't get hung up and not tie a fly because you don't have the exact materials specified in the recipe: make substitutions. If you don't have urine-stained red fox underbelly fur (who does?), then use reddish-tan rabbit or another fur sub- stitute. And if you don't have any of the fur that comes from between the toes of a snowshoe hare to make the wing of a fly, use a tuft of Antron. No wood- duck flank feathers? Use mallard flank. No cream thread? Then use light tan.

Start Tying Behind the Hook Eye

When tying any kind of fly, start the working thread behind the hook eye rather than at the bend. Lock the thread in place with a small drop of cement, and wrap a layer of thread on the shank. Placing a thread base on the shank prevents materials from shifting on the hook and produces a stronger fly.

Fly-Tying Style

Examine these three classic wet flies tied by Dick Talleur. Although they are
different patterns, they were obviously all made by the same tier. The length
of the wings, tails, and throats are all the same; the dimensions of the bodies
are identical; and even the tinsel tags in the hook bends of two of the flies
look the same. Dick is a master tier, and he never lashes materials to hooks in
a haphazard fashion; he carefully uses the same proportions to give his flies a
polished, professional look.

*Noted fly-tying authority, author, and lecturer Dick Talleur made
these three beautiful wet flies.*

On the Water: Tips for Caring for
Your Flies When Fishing

Selecting and Finding the Best Flies

You can always spot a veteran angler by the way he approaches the water: he doesn't dash in and start flailing with his fly rod, he takes some time to study the river. He sees if there are any rising fish, and he tries to determine what they are eating. But what if the fish are not rising? What then?

Take a few minutes to study the stream-side foliage, especially the undersides of the leaves. You'll often find mayflies, caddisflies, and other insects clinging to the vegetation, waiting for their time to return to the water to mate. And examine the trunks of trees and rocks for the spent cases of stonefly nymphs. Select nymph and emerger imitations to match the insects you discover.

This simple sleuthing is critical to developing your skills as a fly tier. Note the sizes, shapes, and colors of the insects you find along the banks of your favorite waters. This information is invaluable for creating convincing imitations.

Comb Your Hair While Fishing

Carry a small comb when fishing. Use the comb to untangle the hair on saltwater flies.

Open Your Fly Box After Fishing

You wouldn't store away a fine bamboo fly rod wet, would you? The same holds true for your flies. Get in the habit of leaving your boxes open overnight to allow moisture to evaporate. Even the moisture from just a couple of flies that you fished will raise the humidity in a closed box and cause all the hooks to rust.

Desiccant Packs Protect Flies

Save the small desiccant packs that come with clothes and other packaged items. Pin one of these packs in your fly box to absorb moisture and prevent hooks from rusting.

Don't Carry Hundreds of Flies

A fly box filled with hundreds of flies, lined up like an army ready for inspection, is a glorious thing to behold. But a box full of well-tied flies discolored by rusting hooks will break your heart: hundreds of hours of labor, and perhaps an equal amount of money in materials, all lost. Store your army of flies in a large fly box that you leave in the car or cabin, and carry only a platoon of flies—a well-rounded selection of the patterns you will most likely use—into battle with the fish. If necessary, you can always return to your large stash of flies to get reinforcements.

CHAPTER 2

Material Matters

Prep the Materials Before Tying

Tying flies is a lot like cooking a meal: prepping the ingredients speeds the process and makes it more enjoyable. Count out the hooks, hackles, and other materials. Trim the feathers and other materials to length. Then start tying the flies.

Organize Your Materials to Save Time

Develop a system of organizing your materials on your tying desk. Keeping everything organized will save you time. Production fly tiers usually lay out materials in the order in which they will be tied to the hooks. That's a valuable tip we can all use to make our tying more efficient.

Cover Materials Between Tying Sessions

A rectangular plastic party veggie or cake cover is ideal for covering your tying area to keep dust and pet hair off thread, floss, and other materials when not tying for a couple of days. A pillowcase or other piece of cloth is also ideal for covering your tying area.

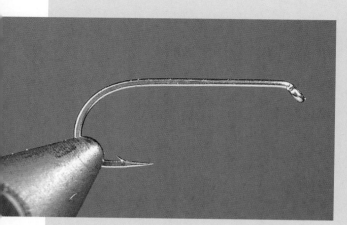

The Hook as a Measuring Device

You can use the hook to judge the proportions of the parts of a fly: the size of the body, the length of the tail and wing, and so on. Take this common dry-fly hook: There's the overall length of the hook, the length of the hook shank, the width of the gap, and the distance between the hook point and the tip of the barb. You can use any of these dimensions to gauge the length of the parts of the fly you'd tie on it. The spot on the hook shank opposite the hook point and hook barb are also good reference points for tying the tail and body of the fly. Follow these dimensions when changing hook sizes, and all of your patterns will have the same proportions.

The hook is the chassis of the fly. It is also a handy measuring device. Study this common dry-fly hook, and think of all the different dimensions you can use to measure the parts of a fly.

Finishing a Thread Head With Super Glue

Finishing a head with Super Glue welds the threads together. Start wrapping the head, apply a drop of Super Glue, and complete wrapping the head. Next, secure the thread with a half hitch and snip. You may apply another tiny drop of Super Glue, but it really isn't necessary.

A Smooth Base Over Lead Wire

In order to wrap a neat, level body, you must first create a level underbody. This is particularly difficult when wrapping lead wire. Use the tapered end of a bodkin to smooth the ends of the wire after you have wrapped it around the hook. Another option is to wrap thread at each end of the wrapped wire. Taper the thread from the wire to the hook shank, especially at the butt end of the fly.

Add More Wax to Pre-waxed Thread

Today's tying threads are usually called "pre-waxed," but there is really not much wax on the thread. For many tying operations, such as tying on wings, pull the thread through a piece of hard tying wax. Tacky thread will stay on the hook shank when wrapped and is less likely to slip or unwrap when bobbin pressure is released.

Preventing the Thread From Slipping Off the Hook

Instead of positioning the hook in the vise with the shank parallel to your bench top, place the hook with the eye slightly above the bend. This helps prevent the final thread wraps from slipping forward and off the hook eye. This is especially handy if you've crowded the hook eye while tying the fly.

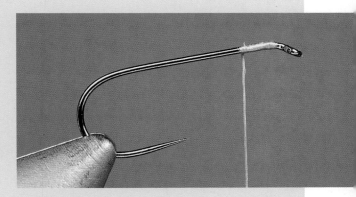

Place the hook in the vise with the shank pointing slightly up to prevent the thread from falling forward off the hook eye. Don't worry about the angle of the thread and the hook shank; it won't hinder your tying.

This brightly colored bead-head pattern is tied on a Dohiku barbless hook. The curved point is the latest innovation in barbless hooks.

Barbless Hooks

Check out the assortment of barbless hooks the next time you're at the fly shop. Some manufacturers are offering barbless hooks with curved points. The curve makes it more difficult for a fish to come off the hook; you have to slightly turn the hook to remove the point from the mouth of the fish. These new hooks do less damage to the fish and will increase your catch rate.

Eliminate Static Electricity

Static electricity can be bothersome when tying with hair or foam. Eliminate static electricity by wiping your hands, hair stacker, and materials with a fabric softener dryer sheet.

Remove Static Electricity From Flash Material

Static electricity makes flash material hard to handle. If this happens to you, run the material through your lips or moistened fingertips. This will remove the static and make the material easy to use.

Mothballs Protect Natural Materials

Toss a couple of mothballs in each bag of natural materials to prevent insect infestation. If you have some natural material that is not in a bag, place the material in a freezer bag and toss in the mothballs. This is especially important with feathers, even if they're on tanned skins; the insects may not like chewing on the skins, but they'll happily feast on the expensive feathers.

Water on Your Bench

Keep a glass of water on your fly-tying bench. Lightly dipping a finger in the water often helps you get a better grip on materials or straighten crooked feathers. Lightly moistening the ends of materials such as marabou, schlappen, Craft Fur, and Krystal Flash before tying to the hook does wonders to tame unruly ingredients.

Spin Dubbing Counterclockwise

When tying a dubbed body, spin the dubbing counterclockwise on the thread. The dubbing will continue twisting tightly around the thread when you wrap the material up the hook. This technique increases the durability of a dubbed body.

Dubbing Amounts

Knowing how much dubbing to spin on the thread when making a dubbed body is one of the most difficult things to learn. It takes a lot of practice and even then you'll make mistakes. It's best to select the amount of dubbing you think you will need to make the body of the fly, and then divide it in half. Spin that small pinch of dubbing on the thread. If you need more dubbing, spin a wisp more on the thread and wrap the body. Remember: It's always easier to add dubbing to the thread than it is to pick the fur off the fly after wrapping the body.

Bay Leaves Deter Pests

There are many organic repellents that will protect your valuable tying materials from pests. Bay leaves are a simple, safe way to keep pests from invading your stash of fly-tying materials.

Look for bay leaves in the spice aisle of your local grocery store. They are a natural way to keep insects from invading your fly-tying materials.

Increasing the Traction of Dry-Fly Hackle

When tying on a dry-fly hackle, clip the side of the feather that will face the hook close enough to create a serrated edge. The resulting traction between this edge and the hook shank or underlying materials will increase the strength of the finished fly; it just might make the difference between a fly that lasts all day and one that falls apart after a couple of hard strikes.

Clip the side of the hackle that will lay against the hook shank or thread base. The serrated edge strengthens the wrapped hackle collar.

Flash Triggers Strikes

A dash of flash often triggers strikes when targeting selective trout. Flashy materials such as Flashabou, Fluoro Fibre, Mylar tinsel, and silver-lined beads mimic the gas bubbles emerging aquatic insects generate under their skins.

Changing the Curve in a Hackle

Many saddle hackles have a natural curve. Sometimes you can make the curve work for you when tying the wing on a streamer, but other times the feather curves in the wrong direction. You can change the natural curve in a saddle hackle by running your thumbnail along the stem of the feather on the opposite side of the curve.

Bungee-Cord Rubber Legs

Don't toss away frayed bungee cord. The small-diameter rubber bands inside a bungee cord make terrific legs for tying flies; one cord contains almost a lifetime supply of legs. And you can color the bands using permanent markers to create a rainbow of different legs.

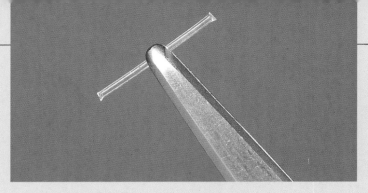

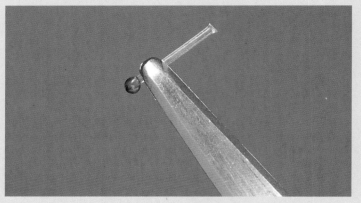

Melting Monofilament Eyes

Do you have trouble getting your homemade monofilament eyes to come out even? Is one eye lopsided when compared with its neighbor? Here's a simple solution for making great melted monofilament eyes every time.

1 Grasp a short piece of 40- to 50-pound-test monofilament with tweezers.

2 Touch a flame to the edge of one end of the mono to start melting an eye.

3 Turn the tweezers over to start melting the other eye. Continue turning the tweezers and melting the eyes. When the eyes get close to the tweezers, place the flame in the middle of the tool to melt both eyes at the same time. Work quickly throughout the entire process.

4 Here are the finished melted eyes tied to a hook. They look perfect.

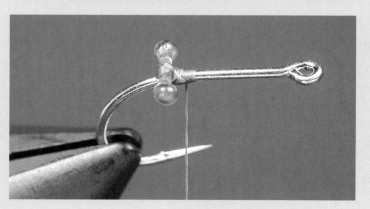

Lint Roller Cleanup

Keep a lint roller on your bench to brush hair and other materials off your clothing when you're done tying.

Change Color of Feathers Using Permanent Markers

Sometimes you can use a permanent marker to easily change the color of a feather to suit your need. For instance, when recently tying a collection of brown and dingy olive damselfly nymphs, I needed some speckled-brown and speckled-olive feathers to tie the legs. I had a coq de Leon hen neck containing lovely mottled feathers, but the fibers on the feathers were gray. A few swipes of a brown marker on some of the feathers, and an olive marker on another group, created the perfect hackles for tying those nymphs.

Tip for Tying Under the Hook Point

When attaching materials to the end of the hook shank, it is sometimes difficult to manipulate the bobbin and thread under the point to catch the material. When this happens, spin the bobbin counterclockwise. When you ease off on the tension, the thread slightly jumps to the rear of the hook. This will help you manipulate the thread over the material you are trying to catch.

Homemade Bead Eyes

Scads of crab and shrimp patterns call for plastic eyes. While many tiers melt small eyes on the ends of pieces of monofilament, you can make a batch of great-looking eyes using glass beads and monofilament. Just thread a bunch of beads onto a piece of 25-pound-test mono. Place a drop of epoxy below each bead, and slide the bead onto the glue; space the beads about ⅛ inch apart. Set the monofilament aside to allow the epoxy to dry. Later, when tying your flies, clip matched sets of eyes from the strand.

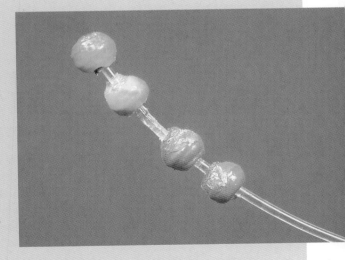

A stem of bead eyes: Clip off sets of eyes as you need them.

Evening the Tips of Squirrel-Tail Hair

There's no need to use a hair stacker to even the tips of squirrel-tail hair. Just stroke the hair perpendicular to the tail; this aligns both the tips and the various colors of the hair. Clip the amount of material you need from the tail.

Pull the bunch of squirrel hair perpendicular to the tail and clip. The tips of the hair will be fairly even.

Adhesive Lead Foil

Adhesive lead foil, which you'll find in your favorite fly shop, is ideal for adding weight to 2X- and 3X-long nymph hooks. A thin strip of foil, wrapped on the hook shank, adds ample weight but creates less bulk than lead wire.

Making Layered Foam

Some flies, such as bass bugs and a lot of large, western terrestrial patterns, call for layered pieces of closed-cell foam. A good cement, such as Best-Test Premium, comes with a brush applicator that makes it easy to construct layered foam. Apply a thin coat of the cement on one surface of each piece of foam and allow the cement to dry. Stick the two tacky surfaces of foam together. Repeat this procedure to add a third piece of foam. Mix colors of foam to create unique foam bodies and heads on your flies.

Making Foam Disks

Some patterns call for foam disk heads and bodies. These disks make the flies float and create fish-attracting noise when retrieved. An empty brass shell casing is an ideal foam cutter; cases from .38 to .45 caliber are perfect for this purpose. Sharpen the open end of the casing with emery paper. Place the casing on the thin sheet of foam, and tap it with a hammer. The casing will punch out a perfect disk every time.

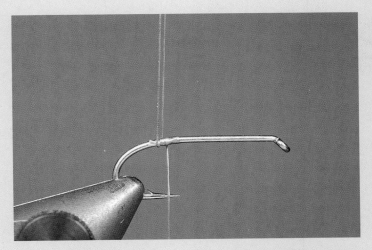

Dubbing Loop Over the Hook

Most tiers apply dubbing to a dubbing loop *under* the hook. Try adding dubbing to the loop *over* the hook. This method avoids interference from the vise and hook point. Make the loop above the hook, add the dubbing, and close the loop. Pull the loop below the hook. Now you can spin the loop closed. (This tip is useful for tiers who do not have rotary vises. If you use a rotary vise, just rotate the hook until the point is on top, and make the loop pointing down.)

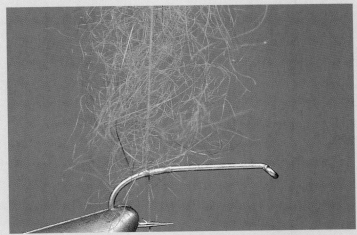

1 Make the dubbing loop on top of the hook.

2 Fill the loop with dubbing. Note how the hook point does not interfere, and I can easily place dubbing against the shank.

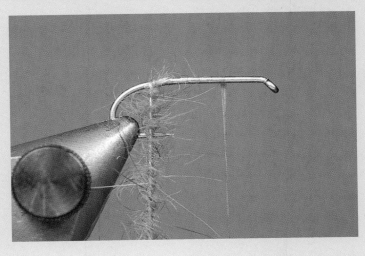

3 Pull the loop under the hook and twist closed. I'm now ready to wrap the dubbed body of the fly.

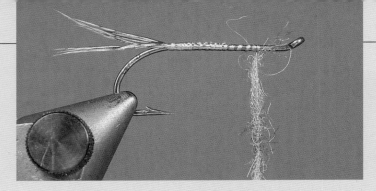

Multi-Layered Dubbed Bodies

When dubbing a thick body, use two thin layers of dubbing instead of a single heavy layer. Make a dubbing loop or spin dubbing on the thread at the front of the fly. Wrap the dubbing to the end of the hook and then back to the beginning.

1 Spin a pinch of dubbing on the thread.

2 Wrap the dubbing to the base of the tail of the fly.

3 Spin another pinch of dubbing on the thread.

4 Wrap the dubbing back up the hook to complete the body of the fly. This layered method is particularly useful when tying larger dubbed bodies.

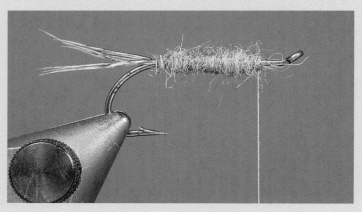

Mylar Tubing That Does Not Fray

Mylar tubing is maddening to use: the stuff always seems to fray when you tie it to the hook. Here's a solution that will keep your nerves from fraying, too:

First, remove the cotton core from the tubing. Next, spray the inside of the tubing with cheap hairspray. Allow the spray to dry and then tie the fly. The hairspray acts as an adhesive and keeps the tubing from fraying.

Cutting Strips

A round, handheld rotary cutter, similar to a pizza cutter, is great for cutting foam strips, as well as narrow strips of Thin Skin and similar materials. Place a straightedge on the foam, and slice with the cutter. Look for one of these nifty tools in your local craft store. Buy the self-healing cutting mat that is often sold near these cutters or sold with a cutter as part of a package deal.

Cutting Sheet Body Materials

Cutting thin, straight strips of sheet body materials can be tough. Sandwich the sheet of material between two pieces of paper, and cut perfect strips in a paper cutter.

Prevent Floss from Fraying

Moisten floss by wetting your fingers before you wrap the material on the hook to minimize fraying. Keep moistening it as you wrap too. Another option is to place the spool of floss in a bobbin to avoid touching the material with your bare fingers.

Offset Hooks Catch More Fish

When tying a very small fly, slightly bend the hook point to the right or left. An offset hook will increase your number of hookups. Always bend the hook prior to tying the fly in case it breaks. This is also an excellent time to crimp the barb.

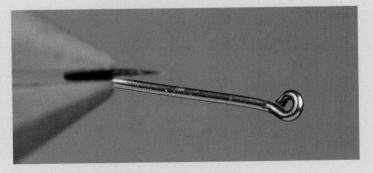

I have gently bent the business end of the hook to one side. This offset will increase hookups.

Head Cement and CDC Do Not Mix

When you finish a fly, you usually put a small drop of cement on the head to seal the thread knot. Cul de canard, however, easily wicks up the cement, which will destroy its unique floating properties. Whenever you tie with CDC, use only a very small drop of cement and keep it well away from the feather.

Moistening Marabou

It's standard procedure to moisten marabou before tying it to the hook to form the wing or tail on a fly. But the fibrous outer pieces of marabou hold the moisture and make it difficult to control the inner pieces of feather. Place a small drop of dishwashing soap on a saucer. Dip your finger in the soap, and brush it on the marabou. The soap breaks the surface tension of the marabou and makes it easier to moisten all the fibers.

Which End of the Peacock Herl?

I prefer tying the butt end of a peacock herl to the hook and then wrapping the herl body or butt of the fly. If you wish, you can tie on and wrap the tip end. The very tip of the herl, however, is too frail for tying flies and should be discarded. Measure about a quarter of the way from the tip and clip. Then tie the remainder of the herl to the hook and continue tying the fly.

Freezer Bags for Storing Materials

It finally came to the point where I couldn't stand it anymore: I had so many fly-tying materials that I could no longer find anything, and my tying had almost come to a complete standstill. I had tubs and tubs of materials everywhere. The tubs were labeled to identify their contents, but I always had to put everything back into its assigned tub after tying, and frankly, I'm not that organized. When I tie flies, I want to spend my time making things that catch fish, not managing my materials collection. Freezer bags solved this problem.

Rather than storing materials in tubs, I now use quart and gallon freezer bags. Using the clear plastic bags allows me to see their contents and I can quickly find what I need, when I need it. I have bags for chenilles, bags for tailing materials, bags for hooks. I then mounted all the bags on a pegboard above my tying bench. I can now easily find what I need, and I spend more time actually tying flies.

Aligning Calftail Hair

Calftail hair is naturally crinkled, and it is difficult to even the tips in a hair stacker. Some of the hairs will be too long and some too short. Instead of using a hair stacker, stroke the hair perpendicular to the tail and cut a slightly larger amount than you need. Remove about a third of the longest hairs and align the tips of the remaining two-thirds. Next, grab the tips of the bunch, and brush out and discard the shortest hairs. This leaves a nice bunch of reasonably aligned hairs.

Squirrel tail hair is a very common fly-tying material, but you must take extra care to lock it firmly to the hook. The wing on this lovely salmon fly was made using dyed squirrel tail hair. This pattern, called the Bush Pilot, was tied by Maine's Charlie Mann.

Hard Hair

Some materials, such as calf and squirrel tail hair, do not compress under thread tension. We call these "hard" hairs. There is a tendency for hard hair to move out of position and loosen when you lift and trim the butt ends. One solution is to clip the hair to length before tying it to the hook. Add a drop of Super Glue to the thread wraps to lock the hair to the hook.

Better Baitfish Backs

The dark blue crest feathers from a silver pheasant make absolutely fantastic backs on any baitfish pattern with a dark back. The feathers naturally come in different lengths, and there are very few other uses for these lovely feathers.

Blended CDC Dubbing for Buggy-Looking Flies

Mix cul de canard fibers with hare's mask fur to create a dubbing that traps tiny air bubbles and gives your flies a truly buggy look. This is a common practice among European fly tiers.

Homemade Adhesive Eyes

A handheld hole punch is great for making adhesive Mylar eyes. Punch out the eyes from a sheet of adhesive-backed Mylar, and make the pupils using a toothpick broken in half and dipped in black paint. Stick the eyes on the sides of the head of the fly, and coat them with drops of cement or epoxy to protect the painted pupils.

Tying Flash on a Fly

When tying flash material onto a fly, don't tie one piece on one side and then a separate piece on the other side of the fly. It is almost always easier to fold a piece of flash in half on the thread and tie the material onto both sides of the hook evenly at the same time. This creates a perfect lateral line that is very appealing to both other anglers looking at your fly and, more important, to the fish.

Recycled Tippet Material

Some anglers are fanatical about replacing their spools of tippet material, especially monofilament nylon, with fresh spools at the beginning of each fishing season. If you follow this practice, save those old spools for tying flies. Fine monofilament is ideal for making the tails on mayflies and wrapping the bodies on midges and other small flies. Waste not, want not!

Moisture and rough use have erased the size from this spool of tippet material. Rather than tossing it in the trash, you can use it to make tails on mayflies or wrap invisible ribs over fragile body materials.

Cut the Corner of Flashabou and Krystal Flash Packaging

Flashabou, Krystal Flash, and similar materials can quickly become tangled messes after you remove them from their packaging. So why remove them from the packaging? Clip a corner from the package and use a bodkin to pick out only the number of pieces of material you need to tie a fly. The remaining material remains neat and untangled.

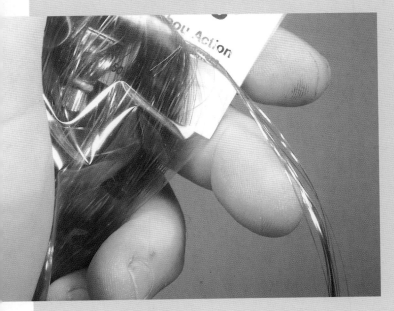

Clip the corner from the package of Flashabou or similar material. Pick out only the pieces of material you need to tie the fly. The rest of the material remains neat in the package.

Reduce Bulk and Save Material

Fold flash and synthetic tailing materials around the thread. Slip the materials on the hook and lock them in place with two or three firm thread wraps. This simple method locks the material in place with a minimum of wraps and reduces waste because you'll only need half the strands of material to tie the fly and there is less excess to trim away.

Don't Waste Material

Tie materials to the hook by their short tag ends. This will eliminate having to cut and waste a lot of excess material and will prevent accidentally cutting the thread when trimming unwanted material.

Soak Quills Before Wrapping

Stripped quills, commonly made from saddle hackles, are a traditional fly-tying material. The trick is to soak the bare quills in a small bowl of water before using to prevent them from cracking or splitting when wrapping on the hook.

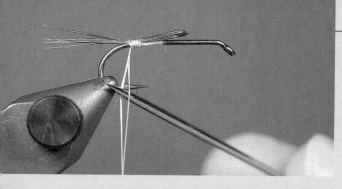

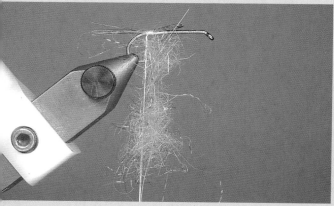

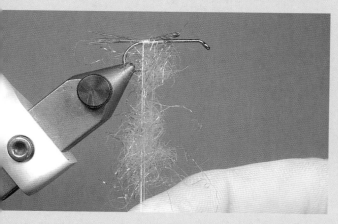

Split-Thread Dubbing Method

If you've learned to apply dubbing using a dubbing loop, the split-thread method will revolutionize your fly tying. It's particularly effective when working with fine-fibered dubbing, rabbit dubbing, and blends; it doesn't work as well with heavy fibered dubbing such as angora. Note that this method works only with flat-waxed types of thread such as UTC; it does not work with UNI-Thread.

1 Secure the thread with a half hitch; as you'll see in a moment, this is important! Next, when wrapping the thread while tying the fly, put one twist in the thread with each new wrap. Spin the bobbin counterclockwise to remove the twist; the fine thread fibers should hang straight and not twist. Carefully split the thread using your sharp bodkin.

2 Insert a pinch of dubbing in the thread. You may raise the bobbin to release the tension on the thread; this sometimes helps to split the thread in two. The half-hitch knot you tied in step 1 keeps the fly from coming apart when you release the tension.

3 Pinch the thread below the dubbing. Raise your pinched fingers and the thread toward you, away from the hook point. Spin the bobbin clockwise. Continue to the next step to see the magic!

4 Remove your fingers and the twist migrates instantly up the entire length of thread and spins the dubbing. I know of no better way to spin fine dubbing.

Bead Basics

If you look closely at a metal bead designed for fly tying, you'll see that one hole in the bead is narrower than the other. Place the narrow hole against the hook eye; the wider, countersunk hole should usually face the body of the fly.

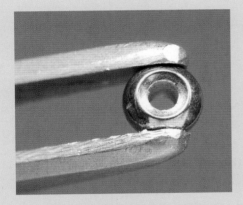

Here are two sides of the same bead. Notice that one hole is wider than the other. The narrower hole should usually face the hook eye, and the wider, countersunk hole faces the body of the fly.

Burning Stripped Quills and Peacock Herl

Do you want to make a batch of stripped hackle quills or peacock herl to tie a large number of flies? Rather than stripping off the unwanted fibers, you can burn off the fibers using a 50-50 solution of bleach and water mixed in a small bowl. Place the feathers in the solution for a few minutes. Monitor the feathers until the fibers are burned from the stems. Quickly remove the stems from the solution and bathe in clean water to remove the bleach.

Making Stripped Peacock Herl With an Eraser

Some classic dry-fly patterns use stripped peacock herl for the bodies. To make stripped herl, look no further than a pencil eraser. Firmly hold a piece of herl on your tying bench, and use the eraser to rub the fine fibers off the herl. Simple, huh?

Peacock Eyes Contain Smaller Herl

When tying small flies with peacock herl, select pieces of herl from a peacock eye. Strung peacock herl is all a uniform large size, but the eye of the feather has herl in a variety of smaller sizes.

Keep Dubbing Wax in Your Shirt Pocket

Dubbing wax works best slightly warm. Keep your tube of dubbing wax in your shirt pocket or someplace close to your body. This slight amount of warmth softens the wax so it glides easily on the thread. Instead of wax you can also use the pink Sortkwik by Lee, as Dick Talleur mentions in *Inside Fly Tying*.

Keeping Hackle Pliable

To ensure strong stems, be sure to store your hackle in sealed plastic bags. Never allow your feathers to dry out and become brittle.

Canned Air for Blending Dubbing

Place small quantities of dubbing in a Ziploc bag; use different colors or textures of dubbing, or add a pinch of your favorite flashy dubbing. Close the bag around the nozzle of a can of compressed air. Blast air into the bag to swirl and blend the dubbing. Add additional pinches of dubbing and blend again until you get the perfect custom dubbing, as Charlie Craven does.

Blend Dubbing in a Jar

Place the various types of dubbing—synthetic or natural—in a jar. Next, fill the jar with water and shake to blend. Strain the mixture, pat the blended dubbing with paper towels to remove excess moisture, and set the dubbing aside to dry.

Moisten Squirrel-Tail and Calftail Hair

Moisten squirrel-tail and calftail hair before tying to the hook. This reduces the bulk of the hair, making it much easier to manage.

Clearing a Super Glue or Zap-A-Gap Tube After Use

When using any type of Super Glue or Zap-A-Gap, keep a 2-inch-square piece of corduroy or denim on hand to wipe the tip of the tube. Next, sharply tap the base of the plastic bottle several times on your desk to help the glue retract down the tube. This forces the glue to run down from the nozzle and back into the tube. Never allow unused glue to harden in the nozzle.

Removing Prism Eyes From the Paper Backing

It's hard to remove adhesive prism or doll eyes from the paper backing with your fingers. Instead, use a bodkin to remove each eye from the backing and place it on the fly.

Multicolored Thread Bodies

Twist two or more colors of thread together to wrap a very slim, multicolored body. Twisting several strands of the same color creates a slender, quill-like effect.

Five-On, Three-Off

Tiers who specialize in dressing fancy Atlantic salmon flies and other beautiful streamers use the five-on, three-off method of tying materials to the hook. This method reduces the bulk on the shank to better tie fine, level bodies.

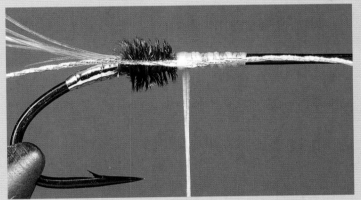

1 Tie the tag, tail, and butt of the fly. This fly will have a floss body and two tinsel ribs. First, I tie on the braided tinsel using five wraps of thread. I tie it on first because it is the last material I will wrap up the hook.

2 Examine this photo very carefully; compare it to the previous picture. I have removed three wraps of thread in order to prepare for adding the next material.

3 Tie on the strand of flat tinsel using five thread wraps.

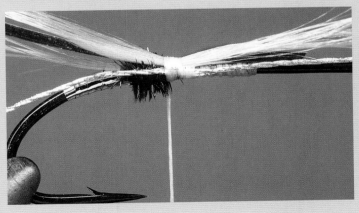

4 Remove three wraps of thread, and tie on the yellow floss. Note the long tags of material: these will create a level underbody. Now you can wrap the thread up the hook and tie the body and ribs of the fly.

Color Stripped Quills With Permanent Marker

When stripping quills—even quills from dark-colored feathers—the bare stems are light colored. I've seen commercially available stripped quills dyed olive, brown, and other popular colors. Another option is to color quills using permanent markers after wrapping the bodies.

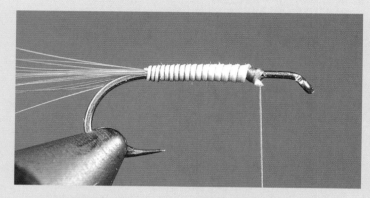

1 Wrap the quill body. Notice how light colored the body is. Let's say, however, that we want this fly to have a brown body to tie an imitation of a March Brown dun.

2 Lightly color the wrapped body with a brown permanent marker.

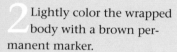

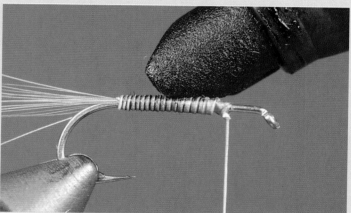

3 This looks like a perfect abdomen for making a March Brown.

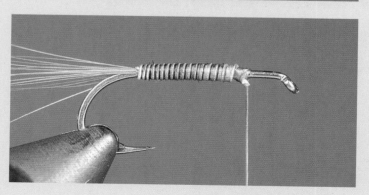

Applying Glue to the Head of the Fly

You've wrapped the head of the fly and whip-finished and clipped the thread. Now you are ready to coat the head with cement. Quickly reposition the fly in the vise pointing up. Next, apply cement to the head. With the fly in this position, the cement will both seal the thread and slightly flow into the materials right behind the head and strengthen the fly.

Neat Head-Finishing Trick

In the previous tip we discussed cementing the head of a fly and allowing a very small amount of glue to flow into the materials. But what if you want to protect the materials from the cement? Use a 1-inch-square piece of 3- to 4-mil plastic sheeting to hold the materials out of the way while cementing the head of the fly; a square clipped from a Ziploc freezer bag works well. Poke a hole in the center of the square and slip the plastic onto the head of the fly. Brush the cement on the thread head. The plastic protects the rest of the fly from the glue.

Exact Thread Placement

Sometimes it's hard to start the thread in a proper position; this is especially true when tying on a curved-shank hook. When starting the thread, reach under the shank with the tag end while holding the tip of the bobbin on the opposite side of the hook. In one motion, move the tag end of the thread counterclockwise while moving the bobbin tip clockwise. Make three wraps with the bobbin to secure the thread. This procedure locks the thread exactly where you want it on the hook.

Other Colors of Nail Polish Create Unique Effects

Where is it written that all flies must have black heads? There are dozens of colors of durable, waterproof nail polish, and you can use these to create unique-looking flies. Silver and gold polish are particularly nice for finishing off saltwater flies and freshwater streamers. Be sure to finish the fly using white thread before applying one of these light-colored polishes.

Black Fingernail Polish for Classy Heads

When tying a presentation fly, coat the thread head with black fingernail polish. Allow the polish to dry, and then apply two coats of clear nail polish. The finished head on the fly will rival the paint job on the finest show hot rod.

Reconditioning Old Hackle Capes

Over time, the feathers from hackle capes can become brittle and hard to use. Hair conditioner will bring new life to an old cape. Massage a small amount of conditioner into the feathers and skin, and place the neck in a bag in a cool place overnight. The next day, rinse the cape and set aside to dry. The conditioner moisturizes and softens the feathers.

Here's a piece of woodchuck fur with some of the guard hairs removed; it looks like I was tying a fly-box full of Woodchuck Caddis, doesn't it? Do you see the tan underfur against the skin? That fine-fibered material makes excellent dubbing. In this case, use the tan dubbing to wrap the body, and the guard hairs to tie the wing on a great-looking cinnamon caddis imitation.

Underfur Dubbing

One of the best dubbings available is a material that we commonly throw away: underfur. Woodchuck underfur, for example, is an excellent dubbing; it has a translucent quality you won't find in many other dubbings. When tying a Woodchuck Caddis, brush out the underfur and store it in a small container. Do the same with any other underfurs that you think might make good candidates for dubbing. Who knows: you might eventually use one of these ingredients to tie a new fly!

Use Baby Powder When Stacking Coarse Hair

Some tiers prefer evening the tips of calftail and similar coarse hairs in a hair stacker. When stacking coarse hair such as calftail, apply a pinch of baby powder to the material before placing it in the stacker. The powder acts as a lubricant on the hair.

Bleached Raccoon as a Substitute for Polar Bear

Although it is legally available, polar bear hair is rather expensive. Bleached raccoon is an excellent substitute.

Reinforcing Peacock Herl

Wrapping peacock herl around your tying thread to make a rope of herl is a good way to strengthen this fragile material. While you can wrap it around your working thread, and then wrap the thread and herl up the hook, here's another idea from fly-tying authority Dick Talleur: Tie the herl to the hook and make a dubbing loop. Next, wrap the thread up the hook to where you will stop wrapping the herl. Cut and remove half the loop, leaving the other half on the loop hanging from the hook. Spin the herl around the hanging strand of thread and wrap the herl rope up the hook. Finally, tie off and clip the excess herl and reinforcing strand of thread.

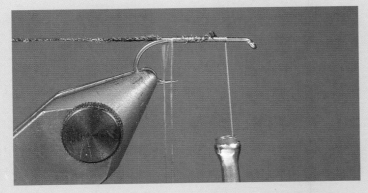

1 Tie the peacock herl to the hook. Next, make a dubbing loop at the base of the herl. Wrap the thread up the hook.

2 Clip away half of the dubbing loop. Twist the herl around the remaining single strand of thread.

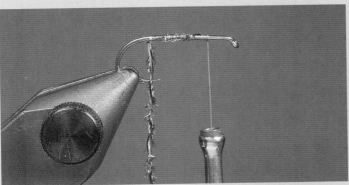

3 Wrap the twisted herl and thread up the hook and continue tying the fly. The reinforcing thread protects the herl from breaking and unraveling when fishing the fly.

Cleaning Dubbing Wax

Does the top of your dubbing wax occasionally get dirty? Do small chunks of wax break off onto your tying thread? Then it's time to clean and renew your tube of dubbing wax. Al Beatty offers a simple solution: swipe the wax on a piece of paper. This wipes away any dirt and debris adhering to the tacky wax, and it repairs the fine slices that occur when you rub the wax on the thread before applying the dubbing.

1 Here's a well-used stick of dubbing wax. It's a simple matter to restore it to almost new.

2 Screw the wax back into the tube until only about 1/16 inch of wax extends above the rim. Swipe the wax on a piece of paper and clean any wax and accumulated debris from the edge of the tube.

3 Here's the restored dubbing wax, ready to tie more flies.

Inexpensive Tubes for Flies

Tying tube flies has become very popular. Plastic-handled Q-tips are an ideal source of inexpensive tubes. Just snip off the cotton ends and clip the tubes to length for the flies you wish to make.

The Floating Smelt is one of my favorite tube flies. This pattern imitates a wounded baitfish floating on the surface of the water. We use this fly to hammer big landlocked salmon where I live in Maine, and some of us play a game of trying it wherever we fish. So far it has taken a wide variety of saltwater fish (I think it was originally designed as a saltwater fly), Atlantic salmon, freshwater bass, and many other species. I guess big fish do eat little fish, especially hurt, helpless little fish. Join the club: tie the Floating Smelt, and try it for a few casts wherever you travel and fish!

Egg Yarn From Craft Stores

In the spring, landlocked salmon near where I live feast on the eggs of spawning suckers; I always see a salmon or two hanging several feet below a group of these mating trash fish. My local fly shop, however, did not carry egg yarn; few anglers in Maine tie egg patterns. I discovered the ideal substitute, however, in the yarn bins at Walmart. For only a few dollars, I bought a lifetime supply of yarn in hot orange, hot red, peach, and flesh tone.

Extension Cord for Fine Copper Wire

An old extension cord is a source for a lifetime supply of fine copper wire that is ideal for making ribs on small wet flies and nymphs; just peel off the plastic coating to reveal the copper. Many hardware stores sell lamp and extension cord by the foot; you can usually purchase a foot of wire for less than a buck.

Stronger Wool Heads

When tying wool heads on sculpin imitations, place a small amount of Zap-A-Gap on the thread base prior to tying on the wool. The glue helps keep the wool from pulling out from under the thread wraps.

Select Materials Wet

Most natural materials turn color and become darker when wet. If you really want to tie flies that closely match the appearance of the real insects, then you should moisten the materials you are considering using. Often-times it is better to tie a fly a shade or two lighter in color knowing that it will turn darker when you fish it.

Pull-and-Clip Method of Trimming Materials

When trimming rubber, latex, and any other elastic ingredi-ents, lightly pull the material, place the scissors against the fly, and clip. The excess tag end will spring back against the thread wraps and be virtually unnoticeable and create no excess bulk.

Thread Spiral-Wraps Protect Fragile Body Materials

To increase the durability of a body made using pheasant tail fibers or other fragile materials, spiral-wrap the thread back to the tail and then forward over the body before mak-ing the tinsel or wire rib. These widely spaced wraps, espe-cially if you're using size 8/0 (70 denier) thread in a color that matches the body, are almost unnoticeable and greatly increase the durability of the finished fly. Use a similar trick to make a dynamite two-tone nymph or dry-fly body. For example, tie a BWO Parachute using olive thread and gray mallard-flank fiber for the abdomen. Wrap the flank fibers on the hook as a body, and then spiral-wrap the thread back and forward over the fibers to create a segmented appear-ance and increase the strength of the fly.

Painting Platform for Dumbbell Eyes

You can buy painted dumbbell eyes, or buy plain eyes and paint them yourself. Make slits in a piece of corrugated cardboard and push the eyes into the slits. Paint the eyes and allow them to dry. Next, reverse the eyes in the slits to paint the other half of the dumbbells.

A piece of corrugated cardboard is an ideal plat-form for painting dumbbell eyes.

Two-Toned Dumbbell Eyes

Two-toned dumbbell eyes will give your flies a custom look. Place the dumbbells in a cardboard shoebox. Spray the dumbbells with paint. Allow the paint to dry, and tap the box to cause the dumbbells to roll over, and paint the other side. Once again, allow the paint to dry. Finally, spray the dumbbells with a second color, and allow this coat of paint to dry. Presto: two-tone dumbbell eyes.

Placing Beads on the Hook

Use your vise as a third hand to place a bead on the hook. Mount the hook with the point facing upright. Grasp the bead in bead tweezers and slip it on the hook. Next, open the vise, slip the bead to the hook eye, and place the hook in the normal position for tying. Better yet, place the beads on a batch of hooks and then tie the flies.

Making Barred or Hot-Tipped Marabou

Make barred or hot-tipped marabou using permanent markers. Lightly moisten a marabou feather and stroke and flatten the fibers. Gently color stripes or the feather tip using the marker. Make the lines as thin as possible because the ink will wick into the marabou as the feather dries.

Add Flash to Stretch Tubing

Stretch tubing is hollow tubing used to tie the bodies of smaller flies and the ribbing on some larger patterns. Use a bobbin threader to pull a piece of Krystal Flash, thin Flashabou, or Ultra Wire into a piece of tubing. The flash material gives the tubing a glow and brightens the finished fly.

Making Hot-Tipped Rabbit Strips

Rabbit strips with hot-colored tips—chartreuse, fire orange, or fluorescent red—add a bit of fish-attracting zip to bunny-strip Matukas and bass patterns. Making a multicolored rabbit strip is so simple you may never make plain-colored flies again. Simply glue a short piece from a bright-colored rabbit strip to the tip of a longer strip. Bond the pieces together—leather side to leather side—using Super Glue.

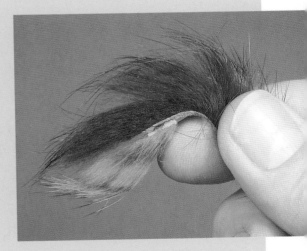

The hot-colored tip on this Zonker strip will make a great-looking fly.

Wide-Space Dental Floss

Wide-space dental floss, which is covered in foam, has many uses on the fly-tying bench. Use this foam to tie tapered bodies and the thoraxes on nymphs, or to build up the heads on nymphs. Color the material using permanent markers.

Store Hackles in Small Plastic Bags

Craft stores sell very small Ziploc bags that are perfect for storing hackles. The bags are ideal for creating a traveling tying kit too. Pluck a dozen or so feathers for tying the sizes of flies you might wish to tie on the road. Jot the sizes of the feathers on the bags using a ball-point pen.

Corks at the Local Hardware Store

Your local hardware store is a great place to purchase corks for making popper bodies. The finished flies will look a little old fashioned, but they are fun to make and will still catch fish. Use cork poppers, and you'll be getting in touch with the roots of fly tying and bug making.

The abdomen on this fly is made using Nymph Skin colored with a brown marker and coated with Softex. You can do the same and complete the fly with your favorite style of thorax, legs, and wing pads to create a fine stonefly nymph. You'll be pleased with the results!

Watercolor Markers for Shading Flies

Watercolor and permanent markers are great for coloring the bodies of flies, but you need to protect the ink for fishing; even permanent marker fades with heavy use. Be sure to coat the ink with head cement, UV Knot Sense, fingernail polish, or another sealer to preserve the color.

Fly-tying legend Dick Talleur often ties the bodies and heads of his flies using the same spool of UNI-Stretch.

UNI-Stretch

Fly-tying great Dick Talleur has long recommended using UNI-Stretch instead of thread when tying streamers. Mount the floss in a bobbin just as you would thread. Use the same color to wrap the body and tie the head, or use one color to make the body and switch to black to complete the head. This is an especially valuable trick if you plan to place adhesive eyes on the fly; the larger head made using UNI-Stretch is perfect for mounting the eyes.

Controlling Marabou

Use a short section cut from a straw to control marabou. Slip the base of the
marabou feather into the piece of straw. Continue pulling the feather through
the straw until you have the length you wish to tie to the fly. Place the feather
and straw on the hook to tie the marabou in place. Tie the marabou on the fly,
and remove the straw.

1 Insert the marabou into a short piece of straw.

2 Place the marabou and straw on top of the fly to tie on the wing. The straw makes it easy to handle the marabou.

3 Remove the straw to reveal the finished wing.

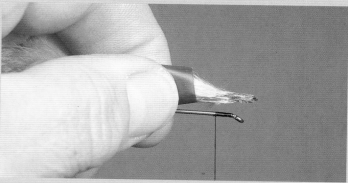

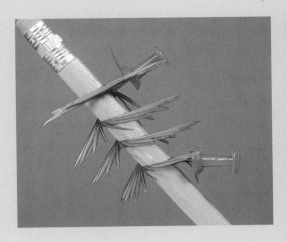

Biot Tree on a Pencil

Biots are short, stiff, spiked fibers that come from the leading edges of turkey- and goose-wing feathers. They are useful for making the tails, legs, and even antennae on larger nymphs, or you can wrap a biot on a hook shank to create the segmented abdomen of a small nymph or wet fly. Spiral-wrap and pin a section of biots on a pencil to make them easier to clip and use.

A pencil is a great way to manage a strip of biots.

Wrapping Over Slippery Squirrel Hair

Squirrel-tail hair is great for tying the wings on streamers. Squirrel hair, however, does not easily compress under thread pressure and is tough to firmly lock to the hook. If the hair in the wings on your streamers slips out from under the thread when you are fishing, try this trick.

Tie the hair to the hook near—but not right at—the hook eye. Place a drop of Super Glue on the base of the wing. Wrap the thread back over the glued area, and then back to the hook eye. Whip-finish the thread and clip. The glue penetrates the hairs and locks the wing to the fly.

McFly Foam for Egg Patterns

Egg yarn is designed for tying egg patterns, but McFly Foam is easier to use. This material is perfect for making extra-large, clown-nose patterns that need a lot of body, and it is also great for micro eggs. On patterns that require thin veils, however, such as the popular Nuke Egg, you have to use egg yarn. Look for McFly Foam in your favorite fly shop.

Coat Popper Bodies With Polyurethane Varnish

After painting a popper body, dip the body in fresh polyurethane varnish. Turn the body and hook until the varnish sets and does not run; this will take only a couple of minutes. Place the hook in a piece of foam or in some other simple device to allow the varnish to dry. The varnish protects the paint and gives the body a deep, professional appearance.

Beads on Egg Flies

Adding weight to an egg fly is always problematic, but a bead is a simple solution. A silver bead gives the fly a little flash, but a red or orange bead imitates an eyed egg.

The talented Anthony Hipps crafted this foam-bodied popper. Anthony painted the body using fabric paint.

Thinning Fabric Paint

Some tiers color popper bodies using fabric paint. These paints are inexpensive and cleanup is a snap. Some paints, however, are too thick for easy and smooth application. Add a few drops of water to the bottle to thin the paint. Test the paint on a piece of paper and add more drops of water if necessary.

Tying Small Bunches of Rabbit Fur

Some patterns call for tying on small bunches of rabbit fur; I have become convinced that swimming-nymph imitations, especially large Drake and Hex patterns, work best if they have tails made using flowing rabbit fur. Tying on rabbit fur, however, is usually a pretty messy operation; cutting a bunch of hair off the hide can result in all kinds of problems. It's much easier to cut a tiny square from a bunny strip and tie the small bunch of hair to the hook with the skin still attached. After tying on a bunch of fur, pinch the butt end between your fingers and clip off the excess with the hide.

1 Tie on a small section of rabbit fur with the hide still attached.

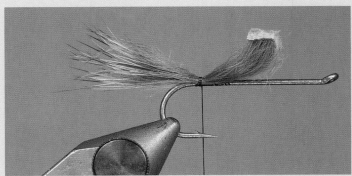

2 Pull the hide until the tail is the proper length.

3 Next, tighten the thread and clip the excess rabbit strip. Use this method to tie the tails on damselfly and swimming mayfly nymph imitations.

Unusual Places to Find Materials

Out-of-Fashion Fly-Tying Materials

When I was a boy, almost all fashionable women wore fur coats and stoles. Today, far fewer wear fur, and you can find discarded fur coats and stoles in almost any secondhand store. But there, too, these garments find few buyers, and you can often pick up a lifetime supply of mink, beaver, and muskrat for a few dollars. Examine the fibers to see that they are still strong, and if they seem fine, buy it.

New Uses for Old Fly Lines

Don't discard that old fly line. Use it to make legs, tails, and antennae on flies. Color the line using permanent markers.

Fur Scraps

Some commercial furriers sell scraps of left-over fur, but others are only too happy to have you cart it off for free. Check the yellow pages to see if you live near a furrier. Call them and explain that you're a crazy fly tier and ask if you could take some scraps off their hands. You'll be surprised how many will welcome your call. A great deal of the material they give you will be of no value for tying flies, but you will find pieces of muskrat and other useful furs.

Synthetic Paintbrushes

An inexpensive paintbrush is a good source of tails for dry flies.

Calling All Hunters!

Your hunting friends can be a great source for natural materials, especially feathers: turkey and pheasant tail, duck quills, and prized wood-duck flank feathers. The fibers from grouse body feathers make terrific legs for small nymphs. Be sure to wash any materials you are given. Store the feathers in plastic freezer bags to prevent insect infestation.

Happy Holidays

Scavenge discarded holiday wrapping for tying materials. Pearl Mylar bows, gold and silver tinsel, Swiss straw, and an abundance of other useful materials are readily available—for free! And don't forget to visit the local discount retailer a day or so after Christmas for the after-season sales; you'll find great tying materials at bargain prices.

It's In Your Underwear

Not to get too personal, but the elastic in your old underwear is a good source of narrow-diameter rubber leg material.

Check out this cased caddisfly tied by Jay "Fishy" Fullum; I originally photographed this fly for Fly Tyer *magazine. Fishy made the case using small glass beads he purchased at a craft store. Stroll up and down the aisles of your local craft store and let your fly-tying imagination run wild!*

Craft-Store Tying Supplies

While it's great to support your local fly shop, many areas do not have one of these unique establishments. Craft stores, on the other hand, are more common. Stroll through your neighborhood craft store to find skeins of chenille, common feathers, foam, and a wide variety of Super Glues. Master tier Jay "Fishy" Fullum regularly finds unique and interesting items at craft stores that he uses to create all sorts of great flies.

Great Tips for Tying With Deer Hair

Antelope as a Substitute for Deer Hair

Antelope hair is a great substitute for deer hair. It's just as durable and often spins more readily than deer hair. Buy a nice patch of antelope if you see it in the fly shop; it'll bring a little variety to your tying.

Secure Deer Hair While You Tie the Fly

Always place a double half hitch after each bunch of deer hair you spin on the hook. Seal the knot with a drop of cement. By doing this small step, you will only lose the layer of hair you are currently working on if you break the thread.

Tease Out Spun Deer Hair Before Trimming

Spin the deer hair on the hook. Next, use your bodkin to tease out the hairs before trimming. You can also use a fine-toothed comb to brush out the hairs. Your goal is to make the hairs stand out as straight as possible for trimming.

Clean Hair Before Stacking

Brush the broken fibers and underfur from a bunch of hair before placing it in the hair stacker. These small bits of material tangle with the hair and prevent the tips from stacking evenly.

Here's the underfur from just one bunch of deer hair. This material would have made it next to impossible to stack and even the tips of the hair.

Deer Hair in Bunches

Spin a deer-hair body in small sections. The secret is to work with manageable bunches of hair about the diameter of a pencil. Don't try to work with too much hair at a time.

A bunch of deer hair equal to about the diameter of a pencil works best for spinning.

Match the Thread to the Hair

When spinning deer hair, select the thread to match the work. If you are using small amounts of hair—a pencil width or less—use Flymaster Flat Waxed 210-denier thread. If you are using three or more pencil widths of hair, use a gel-spun thread.

Best Hair for Bass Bugs

The best deer hair for tying bass bugs is long, straight, and has short tips. The best hair is also thick because thin hair does not have air pockets and will not flair under thread tension. Thicker hair, which is hollow and contains pockets of air, will also float better than thin hair. Examine all the patches of deer hair at your local fly shop with these qualities in mind.

Steaming Spun Deer Hair

Trim spun deer hair with scissors or a razor blade. Next, hold the fly over steam. Any loose and uneven hairs will stand on end. Trim these errant hairs to create a perfect fly.

Best Deer Hair for Spinning and Flaring

Not all deer hair is created equal. The hair along the back and sides of the animal is hollow; it's designed to keep the deer warm during the winter. This thicker hair flares under thread pressure, and it's best for tying bass bugs and the heads on Muddler Minnows. Thin hair does not flare as much and is a great substitute for tying the wings on Elk-Hair Caddises and similar patterns. Deer hair is another material you must examine before you buy. Select hair depending upon the flies you wish to tie.

Working With Glues, Goos, and Other Adhesives

Clean the Hook Eye While the Cement is Wet

You've snipped the thread and coated the head with cement, but you're not yet done with the fly. Push a hackle through the hook eye to clean any cement from the eye. Do it while the fly is still in the vise, and you won't have to fumble around cleaning the hook eye while fishing.

Thread a hackle through the hook eye after applying cement to the thread head. The feather removes any excess glue from the eye.

Is Head Cement Really Necessary?

Head cement is messy, time-consuming to apply, and in many cases is smelly and even mildly toxic. And if applied too thickly or in the wrong place, it can plug up the hook eye or wick into the materials and make them stiff or change their color. Instead, practice making good whip-finish knots. With today's pre-waxed threads, a good whip-finish will likely never come loose. For extra durability, make a second whip-finish over the first.

Super Glue Instead of Head Cement

It's common to apply cement after completing the thread head of a fly, but placing a tiny drop of Super Glue in the head area *before* completing the fly creates an almost indestructible head. Apply the drop of Super Glue and then wrap and whip-finish the thread. The glue welds the thread to the hook.

Measuring Two-part Epoxy

Do you ever make flies requiring epoxy finishes, but the adhesive does not fully harden and cure? No matter how long you wait, and even if you place the flies in a warm place to dry, the epoxy always looks slightly cloudy and feels tacky. The problem is almost always due to improperly measuring equal parts of resin and hardener. Rich Goodman offers a simple solution to this common conundrum. Before squeezing out the two parts of the epoxy—usually on a Post-it Note—Rich traces two circles on the notepad using the cap from a marker pen, a coin, or any other circular object that will give him the correct amount of epoxy. Next, he fills one circle with epoxy and the other with hardener. Now he is assured that the epoxy will harden and cure crystal clear and rock hard.

1 Trace two circles on a Post-it Note pad or index card. Fill one circle with resin and the other with hardener. Thoroughly mix the epoxy and apply to the fly. When properly measured and blended, the epoxy will cure clear and very hard.

2 Here we see the epoxy head on a Surf Candy tied by the great fly tier Bob Popovics.

The Blue-Light Special

You'll find epoxy on the benches of most modern fly tiers—the guys who are willing to experiment with new materials. But epoxy is messy, smelly, and there's always a lot of waste. I've dumped epoxy for most applications and have switched to using Wet-a-Fly Technology's fast-curing acrylic finishes. The acrylic material comes in syringe tubes and is cured using a blue light. Best of all, the material cures in a matter of seconds. Yes, this is the same technology dentists have been using for many years. And best of all, there is no waste; apply to the fly the exact amount of material you wish to use. Bob Popovics now uses Wet-a-Fly's Flex acrylic, which is slightly soft and flexible, to make Surf Candies and his other famous saltwater patterns. I can use all of their acrylic finishes to coat the backs of Copper Johns and even more realistic stonefly and mayfly nymphs. Wet-a-Fly offers complete kits with finish and a blue-light flashlight, as well as separate syringes of material. If you're serious about making epoxy flies, you should check out Wet-a-Fly Technology's line of products. A similar product you'll find in your local fly shop is called Clear Cure Goo.

Wet-a-Fly Technology's line of products are revolutionizing the way we make epoxy flies.

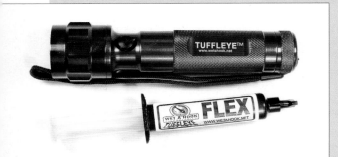

Epoxy and Wood Do Not Mix

Epoxy mixed on wood discolors when cured. Don't ask me why; it just does. Many tiers have had the same frustrating experience.

Use Slow-Curing Epoxy for Making Batches of Flies

Two-part, five-minute epoxy really has very little use in fly tying; the material starts curing once you begin mixing the resin and hardener, and it quickly becomes too thick to get smooth results on flies. For coating the heads or backs on flies, a batch of five-minute epoxy has only about a one- to two-minute pot life. Commonly available two-ton epoxy requires about thirty minutes to harden, so you can complete a larger batch of flies and waste less epoxy. If you wish to tie a really large batch of flies, try using the type of epoxy rod makers use to coat thread wraps; this variety of clear, waterproof glue has a much longer pot life.

Thin Cement for Best Results

Capt. Jim Ellis recommends thinning flexible head cement by at least 50 percent. The thinned cement dries dull, remains flexible, and does not darken materials like some other cements. When tying bigger patterns, use a touch of cement at each step.

UV Knot Sense Substitutes for Epoxy

Patterns such as Poxyback Nymphs and Copper Johns are very effective, but epoxy, which is used to coat the wing cases, is saggy, smelly, sticky, and slow to dry. Substitute UV Knot Sense for the epoxy. Tie a dozen or so nymphs, stick them on a slab of foam, dab UV Knot Sense on the wing cases, and place them in the sun. Presto: beautiful translucent wing cases! Look for UV Knot Sense at your local fly shop.

Serving Cup for Mixing Epoxy

The serving cup from the top of a liquid medicine bottle is perfect for mixing epoxy. After the remaining epoxy hardens, simply squeeze and roll the cup between your hands to break out the old glue and reuse the cup.

Bob Popovics made this trout imitation using Wet-a-Fly Technology's Flex.

Working With Tuffleye Flex

Tuffleye Flex is a pliable acrylic finish cured using the Wet-a-Fly Technology's blue light. Once the Flex is cured, however, you'll feel a slightly tacky residue. Remove this residue using a cloth and rubbing alcohol. Next, coat the Flex with clear nail polish. Bob Popovics has started using Flex instead of epoxy when tying Surf Candies and some of his other famous patterns.

Tips for Selecting and Using
Fly-Tying Thread

Best Threads for Tying Tiny Flies

Selecting the correct thread is critical when tying extra-small flies. Consider using these threads when tying size 22 and smaller wet and dry flies.

- Gudebrod 10/0 (45 denier)
- Euro Thread 12/0 (45 denier)
- UNI-Caenis (20 denier)
- Benecchi 12/0 (70 denier)
- UNI 17/0 (50 denier)
- Ultra GSP (50 denier)

Ultra-fine gel-spun thread is excellent for tying extra-small patterns.

Fishing Monofilament Versus Fly-Tying Monofilament

Monofilament fly-tying thread is *not* the same as monofilament fishing tippet material. It sounds obvious, but some tiers confuse the two and try to use fishing mono to tie flies. Fly-tying monofilament is more limp than fishing mono. Don't bother trying to tie with fishing monofilament.

Coloring Thread With Permanent Markers

If you tie the body of the fly with one color of thread, and plan to finish the thread using a different color, there's no need to change threads. Tie the body of the fly as planned, and when you're ready to make the head and complete the pattern, just swipe two or three inches of thread coming from the hook with a permanent marker of the correct color. Make several wraps of the tinted thread, whip-finish, and clip. You won't have to switch threads, and you'll like the results!

White Thread Under Light Floss

Dark thread will spoil the appearance of a light-colored floss body when the fly becomes wet. Use white thread when tying a fly that has a body made of yellow, orange, or another light color of floss. Switch to a dark-colored thread, or color the thread with a permanent marker, when finishing the head of the fly.

What is Denier, Anyway?

The traditional system of describing the size of fly-tying thread in pattern recipes—A, 3/0, 6/0, 8/0, etc.—is giving way to a more accurate method of rating thread. The garment industry has used the denier standard for many years, and some suppliers of fly-tying threads are adopting it to describe the products they offer. Why make this change?

Under the old system, there was no standard for listing the diameter of a thread, and one company's size 6/0 thread, for example, might differ from another manufacturer's size 6/0. With the denier system, the listed size is based on the weight (in grams) of 9,000 meters of a thread. This improved method leads to greater uniformity so you will know the exact spool of thread to purchase when visiting the fly shop.

Use the following chart when selecting thread to tie the flies you find in books, magazines, and on the Internet.

Size A = 280 denier
3/0 = 220 denier
6/0 = 140 denier
8/0 = 70 denier

Here's a spool of UTC 140, which is distributed by Wapsi Fly. The number 140 refers to the denier weight of the thread and is roughly equivalent to most brands of size 6/0 thread.

Monofilament Thread Requires Two Whip-Finishes

Monofilament thread is slick and is not waxed. Make two whip-finishes whenever completing a head using monofilament thread. Coat the finished head with cement.

Smooth Thread Wraps

Hold the tag end of the thread up at a steep angle when wrapping a thread base on the hook shank. The thread wraps will slide down the tag and easily abut each other, creating a tight series of touching turns.

Use Monofilament Thread to Create Clear Heads

Fine monofilament thread is perfect for tying streamers and saltwater imitations of baitfish. The clear thread allows the colors of the materials to extend all the way to the nose of the fly. Try it: I think you'll like the results.

Test the Breaking Strength of Fine Thread

When using ultra-thin thread, such as 14/0 or 50 denier, get used to the breaking strength before tying any flies. Place a hook in the vise and wrap the thread on the bare shank. Pull on the bobbin until the thread snaps. Repeat this procedure several times to learn how much tension you can place on the thread before it breaks.

Thread Tension

If any tied-in material moves when you increase the tension of the thread (a deer-hair wing is a good example), then you did not use sufficient thread tension when you tied on the material in the first place. When material moves around on the hook shank, it's often because the thread is still stretching and pulling the material along for the ride. Practically every maneuver in fly tying requires using the thread at near maximum tension, which reduces this stretching.

Do the Twist

All fly-tying thread is made with a clockwise twist; some brands are twisted more than others. When tying, you'll increase the twist by half a turn with every thread wrap. Be aware of the twist in thread; it can work for or against you. For instance, if your thread slips or rolls down the head when finishing a fly, it is probably due to too much twist in the thread. Spinning your bobbin counter-clockwise will untwist and flatten the thread.

Protect the Thread from the Hook Point

Do you ever nick and fray your tying thread on the point of the hook? To keep from fraying your thread, pick up some narrow-diameter soft-plastic tubing at a hobby or tropical-fish shop. Snip off a small piece of tubing and slip the piece on the hook point. This will eliminate having to bury the entire point between the jaws of your vise, and it will protect the thread from the sharp point.

Prevent Fraying Fine Thread

Rough fingertips can fray fine thread. This is a particularly naughty problem when using flat-waxed threads. Smooth your fingertips with very fine sandpaper or a pumice stone. You can also apply a small drop of hand lotion to soften your fingertips, but omit this step if you plan to tie with light-colored threads and flosses; hand lotion will discolor these materials and ruin the appearance of the finished flies.

CHAPTER 3

Tool Tips and Tricks

Telescoping Magnet for Retrieving Hooks

Purchase a small telescoping magnet at a hardware store for picking up hooks and other small metallic objects from the floor. The handle telescopes like an old automobile antenna but is usually a bit smaller. On the business end of the rod is a magnet half the size of a dime. If you drop a hook or fly while tying, just extend the magnet and sweep the floor with it to recover the dropped item without stooping over. Carry a second one in your tackle pack for use on the stream to recover flies dropped among the leaves.

A Clean Workspace is a Happy Workspace

Keep a clean tying space. It's incredibly distracting to have loose materials, scraps, and too many tools lying about. Always put away your materials after finishing one pattern and before starting another, and quickly clean your tying bench with a hand vacuum. It was surprising how many experienced tiers recommended this simple but important tip.

Everything In Its Place

Organize your fly-tying bench so that every tool has its own place. The vise is the centerpiece of your workstation, but scissors, bodkin, bobbin, hair stacker, and everything else should have its assigned position. When you need a tool, you'll quickly know where to reach to retrieve it. Return each tool to its home when returning it to the bench. Don't waste time looking for tools; spend your time tying flies!

Coffee Grinder Dubbing Blender

A coffee grinder is a great tool for blending small amounts of dubbing. The whirling blades swirl the dubbing and mix the different fibers. Just don't mix too much dubbing or you might clog the blades, and use the grinder in short bursts; don't keep it running for a long time.

Organize Your Fly Box

Keep your fly boxes neat and tidy, and most importantly, organized. This will help you find the correct pattern quickly streamside, and you'll know what to tie when you get home.

Adjusting Hackle Pliers

Some hackle pliers have a tendency to clip the tip of a feather off while gripping it, thus shortening the hackle to where it might not be useable. If possible, bend the pliers to reduce the amount of pressure between the jaws. Another option is to place a piece of masking tape on the inside of each jaw so the hackle does not make direct contact with the metal tool.

Switch to Ceramic Bobbins

On some plain metal bobbins, the thread goes through a steel tube. Occasionally, the end of the tube will have a microscopic burr that can fray the thread; this is the result of the manufacturing process and is more common with inexpensive bobbins. A ceramic bobbin has a ceramic insert in the tube. The smooth ceramic protects the thread from fraying. A ceramic bobbin usually costs a dollar or two more than a plain steel bobbin, but it eliminates frustration when tying.

The bobbins offered by Montana Fly Company have ceramic tubes. They also come in great camo and trout colors.

Storing Thread on the Bobbin

When you are done tying for the day, slip a half-inch-long piece of soft plastic tubing over the end of the bobbin, trapping the thread against the side of the bobbin tube. This prevents the loose thread from inadvertently slipping out of the tube, and your bobbin will be ready for the next tying session.

A piece of soft plastic tubing traps the thread against the side of the bobbin.

Velcro Material Holder

The hooked side of a piece of Velcro is handy for holding small amounts of natural and synthetic hair and fur. Attach a small section of the adhesive-backed material to the base of your vise. As you tie, place excess hair and fur on the Velcro to keep it from blowing away.

Preventing Screw-On Caps from Sticking

Apply a thin coating of petroleum jelly on the threads of your jar of head cement to prevent the cap from sticking.

Cover Your Tying Desk in White

Place a large, 1/8- to 1/4-inch-thick sheet of polyethylene—or even white poster board—on the top of your tying bench. The sheet will protect your bench from glue and paint spills, and white is a helpful background for tying and makes it easier to find small materials.

Zap-A-Gap on a Candlestick

If you use Zap-A-Gap with any frequency, rather than constantly opening and closing the plastic bottle, put five or six drops in a tiny candlestick holder or a very small glass vial where it will stay fresh for hours. Place the small vial in a wooden clothespin for support. Dip a toothpick in the glue and apply it to the fly.

Using the Bobbin Rest

Many vises come with attachments called bobbin rests. Most tiers toss the bobbin rests in drawers out of sight, and this is a mistake: Bobbin rests are actually very handy devices.

1 First, here's how *not* to use the bobbin rest (top photo). When picking up the bobbin to continue working, there will be several inches of thread extending from the tip of the tool to the hook. That's too much thread for accurate tying.

2 Instead, position the button on the bobbin rest close to and slightly below the hook. Rest the tube of the bobbin—not the thread—on the rest. Now, when you continue tying the fly, only an inch or two of thread will extend beyond the tip of the bobbin.

Clean Your Bobbin Under Hot Water

The wax from thread will eventually clog your bobbin and make it difficult to thread a new spool of thread through the tool. Never use a hard object to clean the metal bobbin tube; this object could scratch the tube and cause thread to fray. Instead, hold the bobbin under hot running water to soften and remove unwanted wax.

Tilting a Hair Stacker

Do you ever have to reverse the hair in your hands after removing it from the hair stacker in order to tie it to the hook? While turning the bunch of hairs, some of the fibers always become misaligned. This is a very common fly-tying problem. The solution is to point the tips of the hair in the direction you plan to tie them to the hook before removing them from the stacker. Now, when you can remove the hairs from the stacker, the material will need less handling to tie to the fly.

Narrow the Fingernail Polish Brush

Much to the chagrin of fly-tying materials suppliers, most tiers use clear fingernail polish as head cement. Before using the polish, clip and narrow the brush that comes on the bottle cap using scissors; be sure to quickly clean the scissors after clipping the brush. This reduces the amount of polish the brush will hold and enables you to apply the polish more accurately.

Protecting Scissor Points

Almost all high-quality fly-tying scissors have tapered tips. The very sharp points are ideal for fine trimming, such as cutting the thread after whip-finishing the head on a fly; you want to snip the thread, not the lovely hackle collar you just tied. When your scissors are not in use, slip a small piece of soft plastic tubing over the blades to protect the tips. There are two rules of falling objects: a jelly sandwich will always fall face down on the dirty floor, and the delicate scissors will hit the ground tips first. I can't help you with the sandwich, but the plastic sheath will protect your best scissors.

Store Materials in Extra-Large Soda Straws

Keep Krystal Flash, Flashabou, and similar materials in extra-large soda straws.

Avoid Round-Handled Bodkins

If you have a choice, buy a bodkin that does not have a round handle. It will roll onto the floor or into your chair as soon as you put it down. Use a bodkin with an octagonal handle (you'll find this inexpensive tool in many fly shops), and this sharp, dangerous object will stay put on your tying bench.

Keep Your Hair Stacker Clean

Keep your hair stacker clean. Most are made of metal, and the inside can become tarnished. If hair does not stack evenly, it could be because of a tarnished interior. Use a cotton swab and metal cleaner to clean it, or an appropriately sized bore brush. Whenever hair doesn't stack cleanly, it's time to clean the stacker.

See Your Work

Get a good magnifier if you're having trouble seeing your work. Many tiers wear simple magnifiers that clip to the brim of baseball caps.

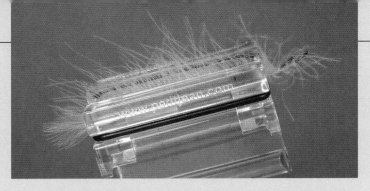

Taming CDC

Want to have some fun with cul de canard feathers? Consider adding Marc Petitjean's Magic Tool to your tying bench. Use the Magic Tool to slip CDC fibers into split flat-waxed thread. Next, spin the thread to form a sort of CDC chenille and wrap the chenille on the hook. To learn more about the Magic Tool and all of Marc's innovative products, go to www.petit jean.com. In the meantime, here's how I use the Magic Tool to tie a simple but very effective caddisfly imitation. This high-floating pattern is deadly!

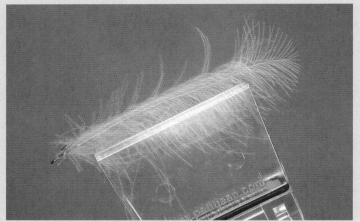

1 Insert the quills of one or two cul de canard feathers into the base of the Magic Tool.

2 Grasp the fibers with the Magic Tool clamp. Open the base to release the quills.

3 Carefully clip off the quills.

4 Start the thread on the hook. Split the size 6/0 (140-denier) flat-waxed thread in two, and insert the fibers. Remove the clamp.

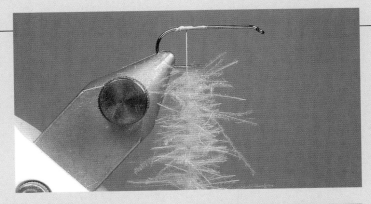

5 Spin the bobbin and thread to make a sort of CDC chenille. (Note the change in the CDC in this photo from the previous photograph.)

6 Wrap the CDC two-thirds of the way up the hook shank.

7 Brush the fibers down the sides of the hook. You may tie on an Elk-Hair Caddis-style wing, but for this fly, I have chosen a burned wing.

8 Wrap the remainder of the CDC up the hook. Make a neat thread head, whip-finish, and clip. Okay, on this fly I showed off and added antennae, but these aren't necessary, and they actually get in the way when tying a fly to the tippet. Omit antennae on the flies you plan to fish.

Velcro Dubbing Brush

A piece of Velcro with the hooks glued to a popsicle stick makes an excellent dubbing brush.

Improved Cement Cap

Push the blunt end of a large needle into a cork, and use the cork as the lid for a cement bottle. The needle rests immersed in the cement. Select a cork that fits the bottle. When you're finished tying, you can replace the cap or use the cork to seal the bottle.

Hair Scrunchies as Spool Tenders

Look for small, elastic hair scrunchies in discount and department stores. A bag full of hair scrunchies is incredibly cheap, and they are perfect for holding tinsel, wire, and thread on spools.

Small, elastic hair scrunchies are great spool tenders.

Hair Straightener for Straightening Feathers

A gentleman once approached me at a fly-fishing show with a great idea for straightening feathers. "A hair straightening iron, the kind you buy at a discount retailer, is ideal for straightening feathers and hair. It works great," he said emphatically. Many thanks to that unknown fellow for this neat fly-tying tip.

Craft Store Templates

Craft stores sell plastic sheeting designed for making templates. Use this material to create templates for cutting Crease Fly bodies and similar foam flies.

Single-Edged Razor Blade a Must

This is simply a matter of personal preference, but a single-edged razor blade is one of the most important tools on my tying bench. I use the blade to cut almost everything: thread, tinsel, excess hackle tips, etc. I lay the blade against the hook, and with one neat slice, cut the material so hardly any bulky tag is left. I use a razor blade far more than scissors for cutting materials.

Template for Trimming Deer-Hair Bugs

When tying deer-hair sliders or divers, which have faces that slope up or down, use a template to trim the face of the bug. Hold the template against the face, lay the scissors against the edge, and clip. A template reduces trimming time and improves the quality of the finished hair bugs.

Hackle Gauge

Having trouble judging hackle sizes? Use a hackle gauge to learn which feather to use on different hook sizes. Some gauges fit right on the stem of your vise so the tool is readily available.

Use a Cup Saucer to Hold Small Items

Do beads and dumbbells roll off your tying bench onto the floor? Is it hard to keep track of small hooks? Use a white cup saucer as a small tray to hold small objects on your tying bench.

Improved Grip on Bobbin

Some tiers wish their bobbins had thicker grips. No problem! Cut a foam hair curler equal to the length of the bobbin grip. Slip the piece of foam onto the bobbin's grip. (Tip: You might find it necessary to wrap a piece of electrical tape on the grip before slipping the foam in place.)

Magnet for Holding Hooks

A magnet, placed next to my vise, is one of the most useful tools on my tying bench. I count out the number of hooks I'll need for a tying session and place them on the magnet. I don't mind misplacing feathers or pieces of floss, but errant sharp hooks, especially if they have barbs, can become dangerous items if they fall on the floor and become lost in the carpet. A small magnet keeps them on my desk.

Fly-Tying Apron

Once upon a time, there was an apron marketed to fly tiers called the Lap Trap. The Lap Trap featured small pockets to hold tools and larger pockets to catch materials and other items before they fell to the floor. Sadly, I cannot find a reference for this item in any catalogs or on the Internet. A cooking or barbeque apron, especially one with extra large pockets, will serve the same purpose. It will also protect your clothing when working with epoxy.

Positioning a Feather in a Wing Burner

There are two ways to place a feather in a wing burner, and both have their advocates; try these methods and see which you prefer.

Some tiers place the feather with the quill in the center of the tool, and then burn the wing; they prefer that the quill run down the center of the shaped wing. Other tiers position the feather with the quill near the leading edge of the burner; they say that this finished wing is more rigid and durable.

With this style of wing burner, the quill runs up the leading edge of the burner.

Dick Talleur tied this delicate dun imitation with burned wings.

Bead Tweezers

If you make a lot of bead-head flies, you'll want to add a bead tweezers to your fly-tying tool kit. The jaws of the tweezers have small dimples that grasp beads so you can easily slip them onto the hooks.

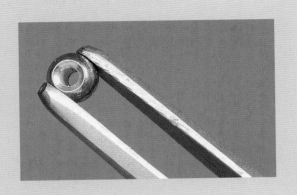

Use Your Bobbin to Make Half Hitches

The tip of your bobbin is a good aid for making a half-hitch knot behind the hook eye. Make three or four half hitches (instead of a more complicated whip-finish), snip the thread, and coat the head with cement. The fly will never come apart.

A White Floor for Retrieving Lost Materials

This tip works best if you set up a permanent fly-tying station in your home or workroom. Place a piece of white poster board on the floor where you will sit, and cover the poster board with a clear plastic chair mat. Now, put your chair on the mat, and resume tying. A lot of the small items that accidentally fall off your bench—hooks, beads, and even finished flies—will land on the mat, and you'll easily see them against the white surface. If your floor is carpeted, especially with dark carpeting, you'll see (that pun is intended) the difference.

Adjust Your Vise for Best Comfort

Be comfortable when tying. This especially refers to the height of your vise in relation to the height of your bench and chair. If you are getting upper back and neck discomfort when tying, the vise is likely too low; if your lower back is bothering you, try lowering your vise.

Multiple Lights for Better Vision

Use a couple of lights at your tying desk. Lighting from multiple angles prevents shadows and glare. Adjust the angle of each light to enhance visibility.

Marking Tools for Easy Identification

Do you attend fly-tying parties or classes where everyone works at the same table? At the end of the evening, all the participants always have to go through the tools to make sure everyone leaves with the things they brought with them. While you could mark your tools with some color of nail polish, I prefer marking my tools with wraps of thread similar to what rod makers use to attach guides to fly rods. Coat the wraps with clear head cement. The thread helps me identify my tools, and it looks a lot classier than hot pink nail polish!

Clothespin for Setting Molded Eyes on the Head of a Fly

Molded 3-D eyes look great on the head of a baitfish imitation. It's common practice to glue the eyes to the sides of the head, but they can be a little hard to hold in position while the cement dries. A spring-loaded clothespin solves this problem. Place a drop of glue on the back of each eye, and press the eyes onto the sides of the head. Place a clothespin on the eyes to hold them in position until the glue dries.

1 Glue the eyes to the sides of the head of the fly. Hold the eyes in position using a clothespin.

2 Remove the clothespin after the eyes dry.

Wooden Hair Stackers

Wooden hair stackers are attractive and very functional. Static electricity can make using a metal stacker difficult, especially in the winter; the hair clings to the inside of the tool and does not neatly slip to the base of the stacker. Static electricity is never a problem when using a wooden hair stacker.

A wooden hair stacker is both attractive and functional.

Scissors for Delicate Cutting

The scissors designed for delicate work have fine blades, hypodermic tips, and lightweight blades. These scissors are intended for use on very small flies and for finishing work. Examples are Dr. Slick's Micro-tips, Arrow Scissors, and small Iris scissors. Don't cut foam bodies for your Chernobyl Ants with these scissors! And stay away from wire, lead, Mylar, and other heavy natural and synthetic materials. These scissors are for tying—not for cutting materials in preparation for tying.

Homemade Bodkins

A large yarn darning needle and cork stopper are ideal for making an inexpensive bodkin. Use the pointed end of the needle to poke a hole in a cork stopper. Next, press the dull end of the needle (that's the end with the eye) into the hole. If you wish, you may place a drop of Super Glue or cement in the hole before positioning the needle, but this probably isn't necessary.

Removing Rust From Your Vise

Fine patches of rust might occasionally develop on your vise. If rust does occur, lightly rub and remove it using grade 0000 steel wool.

Surgical Tubing Grip

Slip a length of plastic surgical tubing onto the handle of a bobbin to improve the tool's grip. You can also slip a piece of tubing onto the handle of your bodkin, dubbing twister, or any other tool with a straight, narrow handle.

Use Scissors Backs to Trim Wire

Good fly-tying scissors are expensive. Try using the back edge of your scissors to trim wire and other hard materials.

Inexpensive Daylight Light Bulbs

There's no need to purchase one of those expensive hobby lamps advertised as recreating real daylight. Today, all discount retailers and hardware stores sell bulbs specifically designed to match real daylight. These bulbs are inexpensive, and they screw right into your favorite lamp. Let the light shine!

Fingernail Clippers

Fingernail clippers are ideal for cutting wire, tinsel, and other hard materials that will quickly dull scissors.

Homemade Tools for Painting Eyes

Some tiers prefer painting eyes on the heads of flies such as Thunder Creeks. Using wooden dowels, sharpened to different diameters, simplifies the task. Dip the tip of a large dowel in white or yellow paint, and dab irises on the sides of the head. Allow the paint to dry. Next, use a smaller-diameter dowel and black paint to add the pupils.

Fortunately, making these tools is as easy as painting the eyes. Cut a 5/16-inch-diameter wooden dowel into 5-inch lengths. Next, partially sharpen the ends of the pieces in a pencil sharpener. Create tips of different diameters to paint eyes of various sizes.

Are Your Scissors Up to the Task?

Most standard scissors are produced using 400-grade stainless steel, and they can handle all natural materials and remain sharp for years. If you tie predominantly with natural materials, almost any scissors can handle the task. Synthetic materials, however, are very hard on 400-grade scissors and can quickly dull or round off edges. Due to this, a whole new group of scissors was designed to handle synthetic materials. Examples are Dr. Slick's Tungsten Carbide, Prism, and Razor scissors. In the case of the Tungsten Carbide scissors, the blades are seven times harder than steel and hold an edge longer. The Prism has a titanium nitride finish that also provides a harder edge. Razor scissors are made from 440-grade stainless steel and are honed to a razor-blade edge for slicing through synthetic materials.

If you tie with natural and some synthetics, most high-quality scissors will work just fine. But if you tie mostly with synthetic materials, consider Razor Scissors or scissors made with tungsten carbide blades.

Plastic Tub to Catch Clippings and Position Tools

Place a plastic margarine tub under the jaws of your vise to catch clipped materials. Cut little notches around the edges of the tub to lean your bobbins, scissors, bodkin, and whip-finishing tool on.

Cover the Hook Point With Fly Line

A snippet of fly line, clipped from the end of an old line, is perfect for covering the hook point. Slip the line onto the hook to protect the thread from the sharp point when tying the fly.

Lubricating a Cam-Action Vise With Dubbing Wax

Cam-action vises revolutionized fly tying; some of today's best vises still use this type of locking mechanism. For better operation and longer life, lubricate the cam on the locking handle with a dab of dubbing wax. Using dubbing wax avoids the problem of oil accidentally getting on fine fly-tying materials.

Squeeze-Glue Bottles as Paint Applicators

Empty cement squeeze bottles with needle applicators are ideal for painting eyes and other spots on flies. Use the micro-fine dispensing tips to put the smallest dots exactly where you want them.

Inexpensive Dubbing Dispenser

Most fly-tying materials suppliers sell collections of dubbing in plastic dispenser boxes. The bottoms of these boxes have holes where you can pick out small amounts of dubbing when tying; there's no need to open the lid to access the dubbing. A small, multi-compartment plastic lure box is perfect for storing your custom blends of dubbing. (You'll find similar boxes at craft stores for holding beads and other items.) Make holes in the bottom of the box using a quarter-inch drill bit, and remove any sharp edges using fine sandpaper. In addition to making a box to hold custom dubbing, you can make another to simply hold all of your favorite dubbings: rabbit, Antron, or whatever. This dispenser will quickly become one of the most important items on your tying desk.

Straight Razor for Trimming Deer Hair

Old-fashioned straight razors are ideal for trimming spun deer hair. Look for these tools in the glass cases in antique shops. Although there's been a surge of interest in classic ways of shaving (frankly, I wouldn't let one of these things near my throat), there is little interest in straight razors at the antique malls, and you will find these items for a couple of dollars apiece.

Plastic Coin Tubes for Organizing Small Materials

The clear-plastic tubes coin collectors use are ideal for organizing tying materials such as custom dubbing blends, beads, dumbbell eyes, and dozens of other ingredients. They are also easy to label (which is a good way to record the recipe of a blended dubbing) and you can see the contents.

Filing Cabinet Storage

A filing cabinet is an ideal way to organize and store many fly-tying materials. Place packaged capes and other flat objects in hanging file folders. Place smaller objects, such as packages of dubbing and chenille, in freezer bags, and then store them in hanging folders. A simple two-drawer cabinet will handle all but the largest collections of materials: place flat objects in folders in one drawer, and store tools and bulky items in small boxes and freezer bags in the other.

Foam Cookie Cutters

Do you tie a lot of foam flies? Foam punch cutters, which work like cookie cutters, allow you to quickly create uniform pieces of foam with clean edges. These tools, such as those manufactured by River Road Creations, will save you a lot of time, and your finished flies will have a more polished look.

Foam cutters come in a wide variety of useful shapes and sizes. Here is a cutter designed for making Crease Flies.

A Cold Mixing Plate Retards Epoxy from Curing

It is helpful to use a mixing plate when tying a large batch of epoxy flies. Cover a small plate with aluminum foil and place the plate in your freezer until it is time to mix the epoxy. The cold plate increases the epoxy's curing time so you can tie more flies and waste less glue. When you are done, just discard the foil.

Store Beads on Safety Pins

Safety pins are great for organizing beads. Fill a couple of safety pins with beads. Close the pins so the beads don't fall off and roll away. Place the pins on a piece of cardboard or neoprene so you can easily find the pins—and the beads —on your tying bench.

Protecting Spey Flies

Oftentimes the most beautiful flies require the most time to tie. Spey flies are good examples of such patterns; it takes extra care to tie the long, waving hackle and swept-back wings. A piece of soda straw, slipped onto the fly, conveniently protects the pattern.

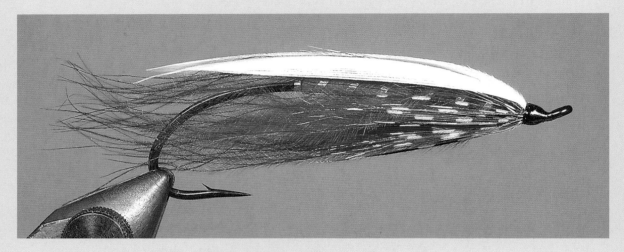

Here we've tied a lovely steelhead Spey fly. It would be nice to find a simple way to protect the wings.

Slip a piece of soda straw onto the fly to protect the wings and hackle.

Homemade Fly Rack

Remove the foam from an old fly box and place it next to your vise. This is the perfect perch for storing new flies.

Plastic Slide Pages for Holding Materials

If you have only a small amount of material to organize, or you're putting together a traveling fly-tying kit, the clear plastic sheets designed for holding 35-millimeter slides have a lot to offer. The pockets neatly hold small quantities of dubbing and many other ingredients.

Magnetized Scissors

Magnetize a set of scissors using a screwdriver magnetizer found in hardware stores. Magnetized scissors are great for picking up dropped hooks and other small metal objects.

An Inexpensive Tool Caddy

Drill holes in a block of foam or wood to create an inexpensive caddy for holding your fly-tying tools. Scissors, bodkins, bobbins, and similar objects conveniently fit in the holes, and the caddy will not damage the sharp ends of pointed tools.

Electrical-Clip Fly Caddy

Look for packages of spring electrical clips at your local hardware store. Drill holes in a block of foam equal in diameter to the base of the clips. Place one clip in each hole. These clips are ideal for holding dry flies, nymphs, and freshwater streamers while the head cement dries.

Barbershop Deer-Hair Trimming

Use electric hair clippers to trim spun deer hair. You can purchase expensive clippers, but the pet department at your local discount retailer has perfectly serviceable—and very affordable—hair clippers. Select clippers with the widest teeth you can find.

Drugstore Bobbin Threader

A dental-floss threader makes a great bobbin threader.

Many Uses for Hackle Pliers

Hackle pliers have uses beyond just wrapping feathers on hooks. For instance, if your thread snaps, grab the broken end with the pliers while you restart the spool. When tying several flies, hackle pliers are handy for holding materials such as a Krystal Flash. Hackle pliers are also great for grasping and spinning the end of a dubbing loop. Over time, hackle pliers will become one of the most versatile tools on your tying bench.

A Small Cutting Board Will Save Your Fly-Tying Desk

Place a cutting board on your fly-tying desk to slice materials with a razor blade or X-acto knife. Cut the materials, not your desktop.

Pen Hair Packer

Use a ballpoint pen, with the inkwell removed, as a simple hair packer. Spin a bunch of deer hair on the hook, and then slip the empty pen onto the shank. Use the pen case to push the hair to the end of the hook. Continue spinning and packing more bunches of hair to make a compacted deer-hair body.

Blending Hair With a Comb

I sometimes see tiers go to great lengths blending different colors of hair when making the wings for streamers. A small plastic comb is a simple solution for mixing hair. Simply stack the different clumps of material—natural or synthetic—and comb them together.

Simple Scissors Sharpening

Use a nail polish bottle as a convenient sharpening stone for putting a fresh edge on your non-serrated fly-tying scissors. Open and place the scissors at the smallest diameter of the bottle. Try cutting through the bottle; allow the scissors to scrape over the glass and then close. Repeat this five or six times to place an acceptable new edge on your scissors.

Favorite Dubbing-Loop Tool

There are a lot of dubbing-loop tools on the market, and I own several. While they all make using dubbing easier, some work much better than others. My favorite tool is brass with a ball-bearing head. The heavy head spins freely and easily twists a dubbing loop very tight. Look for this tool in your favorite fly shop. Several companies offer this style of tool.

The head of this brass dubbing-loop tool is packed with ball bearings. It spins freely and twists a dubbing loop very tight.

CHAPTER 4

Ideas for Tying High-Floating Dry Flies

Thin Packing Foam for Wings

Extra-thin packing foam used for shipping dishes and other fragile objects is excellent for making mayfly and stonefly wings. The easiest method is to shape the wings using a wing burner, but you can also clip the wings to shape. The foam is white, but you can color it any shape you wish using permanent markers.

Two Is Better Than One

When burning foam wings, use two pieces of $1/2$-millimeter foam or your choice of sheet wing material instead of one piece. Lay the two pieces together, and place them in the burner. Melt the edges of the foam to shape the wing. The two pieces of foam, melted together along the edges, trap air inside and increase the buoyancy of the fly.

Look closely and you can see the tiny hooks on the fibers of this cul de canard feather. These small hooks trap air bubbles and make the feather float.

CDC and Fly Floatant Do Not Mix

The fibers on a cul de canard feather contain thousands of tiny—almost microscopic—hooks. These hooks trap air bubbles and keep the feather afloat. When fishing, do not apply any sort of floatant to a fly tied with CDC. The floatant will clog the hooks and prevent them from trapping air.

Best Deer Hair for Compara-duns and Other Mayfly Imitations

Don't use just any deer hair for tying the wings on Compara-duns and other patterns. Coastal deer has finer hair that makes nice wings and creates far less bulk on the hook shank. You will be pleased with the results.

What You See—And What the Fish Sees

Place a piece of Thin Skin on a piece of thin adhesive closed-cell sheet foam. Fashion the wing of the fly. Tie on the wing so that the realistic-looking Thin Skin faces down toward the fish and the bright side faces up so you can easily spot your fly on the water.

Steam Repairs Abused Flies

A dry fly takes a lot of tough abuse. To refresh bent hackle and tail fibers, grasp the hook in a tweezers, and hold the fly over the steam from a boiling kettle. This simple operation repairs all but the most damaged flies.

Thompson's WaterSeal for Flies

Thompson's WaterSeal is a good treatment for dry flies. Dip the flies in the solution, allow them to thoroughly dry, and then place them in your fly box.

A Simple Extended Body

Create an extended mayfly abdomen by inserting Micro-fibetts, hairs, or hackle fibers into the end of a piece of medium Stretch Tubing. Cut the butt end of the tubing to length and tie it to the hook.

Use a piece of medium Stretch Tubing to tie an extended abdomen.

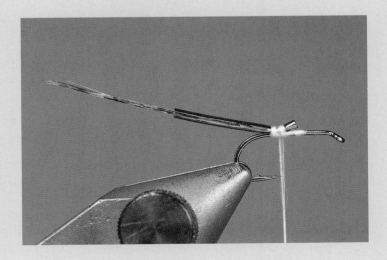

Foam Dry Flies

Foam dry flies have become all the rage out West, but they catch trout throughout North America. Foam dry flies also work very well on the Northeast's landlocked salmon rivers.

Mono Mayfly Tails

Narrow-diameter clear monofilament—such as 10- to 20-pound-test—is ideal for making tails on mayflies. You can even color the mono using permanent markers.

Heavily Hackled Dry-Fly Collar With Multiple Feathers

Using two or even three feathers is the most common way to make an extra-thick hackle collar. First, prepare and tie on the feathers. Wrap one hackle up the hook and tie off and clip the excess. Next, wrap the second feather. Here's the trick: slightly rock the second hackle forward and backward (toward the front and toward the rear of the hook) while you work. This slight rocking motion neatly weaves the second feather through the fibers of the first hackle.

Trimming Hair Dry-Fly Wings

If you do not cut the butt end of the wing at an angle, it will be very difficult to cover the thread wraps holding the wing in place with the hackle collar. Here's the proper way to clip the hair fibers and wrap a neat collar on a Trude-style fly.

1 Tie the body of the fly, and tie on the hair wing. Next, clip the excess wing fibers by placing the scissors almost parallel to and tight against the hook shank. Cut the hair at a sharp angle.

2 Tie the hackle on close to the hook eye. Next, wrap the hackle up the sloping hair base to the bottom of the wing. Leave small spaces between the wraps of hackle.

3 Wrap the hackle back to the hook eye, filling in the gaps between the first set of wraps. Tie off and clip the excess bit of feather and make a neat thread head.

Heavy-Hackled Dry-Fly Collar With a Saddle Hackle

Do you want to tie a high-floating dry fly with a bushy collar? It's not as hard as you think using a long saddle dry-fly hackle. You'll get the hang of this method with a little practice.

1 Tie the hackle on in the normal position. Wrap the thread to the hook eye.

2 Wrap the hackle forward, leaving small spaces between each new wrap of feather. Tie off the hackle with one firm wrap of thread.

3 Wind the thread to the back of the hackle area; take care to not mash down any fibers. Wrap the hackle back to the wing. Tie off the feather with one firm wrap of thread. Wrap the thread back to the hook eye; it helps to rock the thread back and forth while you work.

4 Finally, wrap the hackle to the hook eye; rock the feather back and forth to avoid trapping any of the fibers. Tie off the excess hackle.

Don't make the thread head yet! We'll learn another great trick and complete the fly in the next tip.

A Better Way to Clip Excess Hackle

It's not uncommon to construct a really good-looking pattern and then thoroughly mess it up by making a poor head. The mistake starts with clipping the hackle that is left over after wrapping the collar. Here's a solution to the problem of clipping the hackle and making a neat thread. We'll continue tying the fly we started in the previous tip. First, do not clip the excess hackle against the thread. Instead, hold the feather in place with two firm wraps of thread; I have placed these two thread wraps very close to the hook eye.

1 Brush and hold the excess hackle tip and fibers toward the end of the hook. Wrap the thread to the base of the hackle collar, locking down the surplus feather.

2 Clip the surplus feather, leaving a short stub that gets hidden in the hackle collar. Now you may wrap a neat thread head.

This lovely mayfly imitation has a slender dubbed body. It's one of the hallmarks of an expert tier.

Slender Bodies Work Best

Use fine synthetic dubbing, such as Wapsi Fly's Superfine, to tie thin bodies on midge and mayfly imitations. This is especially important when tying flies for fishing tailwaters. Patterns with bulky abdomens and thoraxes don't work as well as thinly tied flies.

Tying a Split Tail—Method 1

The tails on real mayfly duns and spinners have splayed tails, and so should your imitations. The simplest method is to wrap a thread base on the hook shank; this is also when I tie on the hackle. Next, tie on the tailing fibers. Push your thumbnail between the fibers and the hook to splay the tail. Make a couple of wraps under the tail and tight against the thread base to lock the fibers in position.

Tying a Split Tail—Method 2

This idea takes Method 1 one step further. Wrap the thread base and tie on the hackle. Wrap a small bump of thread at the end of the shank. Next, tie on the tail fibers. Wrap the thread to the bump and tighten. The tails will neatly splay around the thread bump, and you may continue tying the fly. If you plan to tie a body using dubbing, you can spin a very tiny pinch of dubbing on the thread, and wrap this in place of the thread bump.

Tying a Split Tail—Method 3

Start the thread on the hook. Wrap a thread base, but do not clip the thread tag. Tie on the tail fibers. Split the fibers in half using your bodkin, and pull the thread tag between the split fibers. This simple technique locks the split tail in place and adds no bulk to the fly.

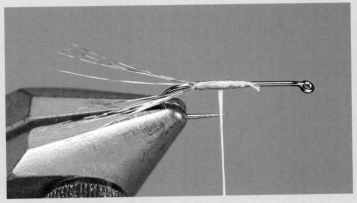

1 Start the thread on the hook. Wrap the thread to the end of the shank; do not clip the tag end of the thread. Tie the tail fibers to the top of the hook.

2 Separate the fibers into two groups. Pull the tag end of the thread between the tails. Tie off and clip the tag.

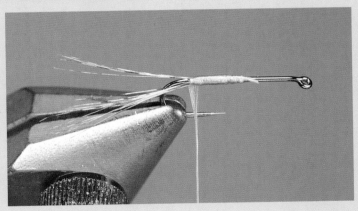

3 Wrap the thread to the base of the tails.

4 Make your choice of abdomen and continue tying the fly.

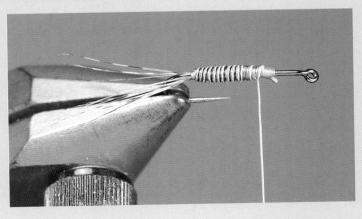

Grizzly-Hackle Damselfly Bodies

Strip large grizzly hackles and color the quills light blue for making the abdomens on small adult damselflies.

Tips for Selecting Elk Hair

It's impossible to believe that there is a trout angler on the planet who has not used an Elk-Hair Caddis. It is one of the most popular patterns and catches thousands of fish each season. Elk hair is used to tie the wing on this famous fly, as well as many other patterns. Here are several tips for selecting the best elk hair.

1 Good hair is hard to find, and harder to buy through the mail because you can't see it before purchase. Always examine all the patches of hair in the fly shop before you plunk down your hard-earned money.

2 Avoid patches containing curved hair; these are hard to use to tie neat wings. Also avoid patches containing fibers with broken tips.

3 Hair that has been dyed or bleached is especially likely to be brittle or broken. Remove the patch from its package to satisfy yourself that the fibers are strong and suitable for tying flies.

4 Not all elk-hair fibers are the same thickness because the different patches of material come from different parts of the animal. Select a patch with fine-fibered hair for tying smaller flies; save the thicker hair for dressing larger patterns.

Wrap Hackle Around Hook to Judge Size

Choosing the correct size of hackle is one of the first steps in learning to tie dry flies. The easiest method is to wrap a feather around the bottom of the hook to judge the length of the fibers. Most tiers like the length of the fibers to equal one and one half to two times the width of the hook gap.

Wrap the feather around the hook to judge the size of the hackle.

CDC Mayfly Wings

Cul de canard makes great wings on mayfly dun imitations. Use four feathers—two for each wing. Tie on the feathers so the wings flair out. This creates a better wing impression and is easier to dry with a false cast.

Reinforcing Raffia Caddisfly Wings

Raffia and Swiss straw are great for clipping wings for caddisflies. These materials, however, tend to split and require reinforcement. Tegaderm, a transparent medical dressing manufactured by 3M, is ideal for reinforcing raffia and Swiss straw. Place the raffia or Swiss straw on the adhesive of the Tegaderm, and clip out the wings. Check your local discount pharmacy for 3M Nexcare First Aid Tegaderm Transparent Dressing.

Mix Hackle Fiber Lengths

Author Bill "Bugs" Logan likes to tie a dry fly using hackle of two different sizes. He says this sort of hackle collar traps more air bubbles and floats higher. Be sure to wrap one feather at a time.

Heating Hackle Fibers to Make a Low-Riding Dry Fly

Rather than clipping the hackles from the bottom of the hook so a fly will ride flush on the surface film, warm and brush the hackle fibers up the sides of the fly. This method accomplishes two things: First, it increases hackle density and allows the fly to float on the surface. Second, the heat lightly crinkles the hackle fibers and makes the legs look more lifelike. Warm the hackle fibers with a lighter; just be careful to keep the fibers away from the open flame!

Reinforced Quill Body

When tying a quill, peccary, or similar body, give the competed body a very light swipe of Super Glue. Now the body will be less apt to break and unravel after the first strike.

Clump Wings Work Well

Rather than tying split wings, a wing made using a single clump of hackle fibers is just as effective. This sort of wing is much easier to tie, and it does a perfect job of mimicking the upright wings of a real mayfly sitting on the water. So stop struggling to tie two wings: just tie one!

Heat-Shrink Tubing Dry-Fly Bodies

Fly tier Dave Cowardin uses heat-shrink tubing to make great unsinkable flies. He heats and seals the ends of the tubing and then ties the tube to the hook to form the body of the fly. Use this technique to form the bodies on grasshoppers and large adult stoneflies; Cowardin also inserts tails in narrow-diameter tubing to craft medium-sized mayfly duns and spinners. Heat-shrink tubing comes in a wide variety of colors and sizes.

Securing Hair Wings With Vinyl Cement

When making parachute-post wings using calf body hair, or divided calf-hair wings like those on a Royal Wulff, the thread often slips off the hair. To correct this problem, apply a small dab of vinyl cement to the base of the post or wings. The cement causes the thread to grip the slippery hair.

Substitution for Wood-Duck Wings

The wings on most traditional Catskill-style dry flies are tied with wings made of wood-duck flank feathers. Real wood-duck feathers, however, are rather expensive, even more so for prime plumage. Try substituting with "lemon" wood-duck flank feathers. These feathers are dyed to imitate wood duck, and the vast majority of anglers—and the fish—cannot tell the difference.

Whiting Farms Tailing Packs for Realistic Tails

For years, chickens have been bred to yield lots of small feathers for tying all sizes of dry flies, including the tiniest patterns. Whiting Farms offers a product called Tailing Packs, which are a good alternative to hackle fibers. Tailing Pack feathers have stiff fibers and come in excellent mottled colors. Try the feathers if you're having trouble finding good hackles to tie the tails on traditional dry flies.

Heavily Hackled Dry-Fly Collar With Two Feathers

Prepare and tie on two hackles. Wrap the first feather in the normal manner—over the top of the hook—and then wrap the second hackle in the opposite direction. This method is especially helpful if you trim the underside of the collar so that the fly rides flush on the surface of the water.

The Hackle Sweet Spot

Pluck a dry-fly hackle from the cape and examine the quill. You'll notice that approximately the bottom third of the stem is thicker than the top two-thirds. The top two-thirds is considered the sweet spot of a hackle. Strip the fibers from the bottom third and use the rest of the feather to tie the fly.

The top two-thirds is the sweet spot of the hackle. Strip and discard the fibers from the bottom third.

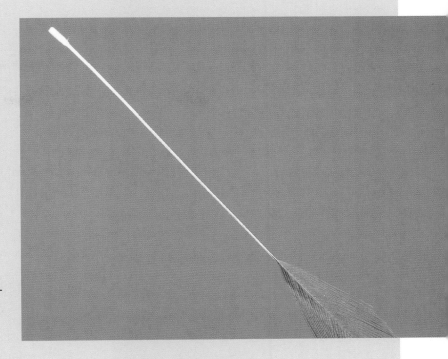

Strip Fibers to Wrap Hackle

You've stripped the fibers from the base of the feather to get to the sweet spot of the hackle. Next, strip a few fibers from the side of the feather that will lay against the hook. I will remove the half-dozen fibers that are sticking out from the side of the hackle. This small bit of bare stem will allow the first wrap of hackle to go neatly around the hook.

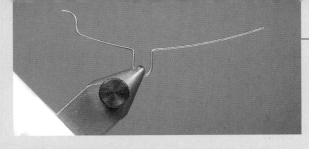

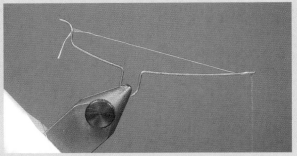

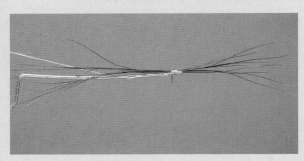

Detached Body Pins for Making an Extended Abdomen

Renzetti, the manufacturer of world-class rotary vises, introduced a product called Detached Body Pins. Use these pins to create realistic, high-floating foam extended abdomens for mayfly, caddisfly, and stonefly imitations. The pins are easy to use, and the results are very satisfying. Use .5- and 1-millimeter thick foam to make slender abdomens. (You can use the following method to make an extended abdomen using a bodkin needle.)

1 Place the Detached Body Pin in your vise. (You do not need a Renzetti vise to use the pin; they work in any vise.)

2 Start the thread on the hooked end of the wire (*on the left*). Stretch the thread to the other end of the pin. Make two or three gentle wraps near the end of the pin.

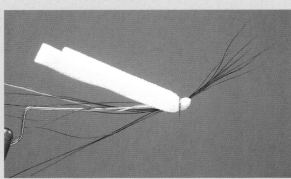

3 Tie your choice of tail fibers to the pin. I'm making an abdomen for a large drake imitation and have chosen hair. (With practice, you can use Detached Body Pins to fashion abdomens for flies down to size 14.) I am not clipping the butt ends of the hairs; these will prove useful when tying the fly.

4 Clip a 1/8-inch-wide strip of foam. Fold the foam under the tip of the pin, and make two of three wraps of thread. This creates the first segment of the abdomen.

5 Spread the foam. Make one wrap of thread up the pin. The second section of the abdomen is made in the next step.

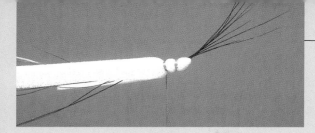

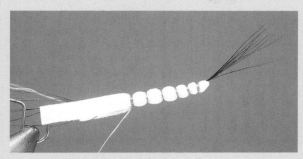

6 Fold the foam against the sides of the pin. Make three thread wraps to create the second section of the abdomen.

7 Work up the pin to complete the abdomen. Repeat the previous two steps to make additional body segments.

8 Use permanent markers to color the foam abdomen.

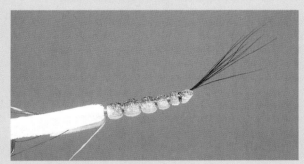

9 Clip the tag end of the thread from the hook. Firmly grasp the abdomen between your fingers, and twist and remove it from the pin. Note that I have not cut off the butt ends of the tail or thread tags. I'll tie all of these to the hook to firmly lock the abdomen to the fly.

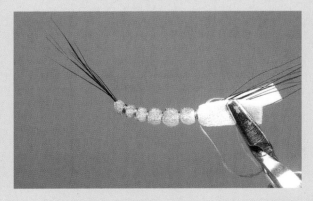

10 Here's a Drake imitation tied with an extended foam abdomen. I took this fly from my fly box to take this picture. I tied a batch of these to match the *Hexagenia* hatch in Maine's Baxter State Park. The flies float perfectly, they are extremely durable, and the fish love them.

Tying Secure Hair Wings

When tying on hair wings, don't let go of the hair until it is secure. Keeping the hair in one neat bundle prevents it from spreading around the hook shank. After the hair is locked to the hook, you can divide the wings in two using figure-eight wraps of thread.

Creating Equal Wing Quill Sections

Use a pair of drafting dividers set to the desired width of the quill sections you wish to create. Separate the sections from the feather using the dividers and clip. Every section will be the same width. Adjust the size of the sections to match the hooks you are using.

Egg Sacs for Dry Flies

A tiny ball of bright yellow dubbing, wrapped on the end of the hook shank in front of the tail of the fly, does an admirable job of imitating the egg sac of a female mayfly.

From the Trout's-Eye View

Examine your new dry-fly creation from below, just the way the fish sees it. How? Fill a clear glass jar with water, and place a mirror at a 45-degree angle in the bottom of the jar. Toss your fly on the surface of the water, and examine its footprint in the reflection in the mirror. You can also place an insect in this simple viewing device to see how it looks to the trout. How your imitation rests on the water is probably more important that its color.

If you take your research seriously, consider purchasing the Trout's Eye View viewing platform. This cool, inexpensive device is designed to examine flies and insects from below. It's a particularly useful tool for tiers who demonstrate at fly-fishing shows and is a wonderful aid when teaching fly-fishing and tying classes.

The Trout's Eye View viewing platform lets you see how your flies appear to the fish.

Preparing Cul de Canard to Wrap as Hackle

Cul de canard, commonly referred to as CDC, has a fine quill. While this quill poses no problem when tying the entire feather to the top of a hook to form the wing of a fly, it often snaps if you try using the feather as a hackle. Fly-tying authority Dick Talleur once shared a simple method for preparing CDC as a hackle.

1 Here's an entire CDC feather. The thin tip of the quill is too fragile for wrapping the feather as a hackle.

2 Grasp the base and the tip of the quill, and give the feather a good tug. The stem will snap at the weakest point, usually about a third of the way from the tip. Discard the tip and use the remaining part of the feather to tie the fly.

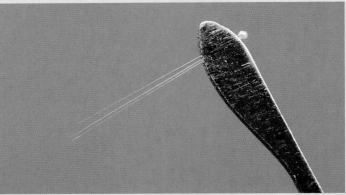

Working With Microfibett Tails

Microfibett tails are great for tying small mayfly imitations, but the wispy fibers are sometimes difficult to control. Rather than tying loose Microfibetts to the hook, fuse the butt ends of the tails with a lighter and then tie the tails to the fly.

1 Grasp the Microfibetts with tweezers or a wing burner and clip them from the bunch.

2 Melt and fuse the butt ends together.

3 Start the thread on the hook. Tie the bunch of Microfibetts to the top of the hook.

4 Pull the tail back until the small ball of plastic touches the thread wraps. Pull the thread tight to lock the tail in place, and continue tying the fly.

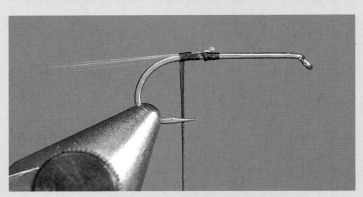

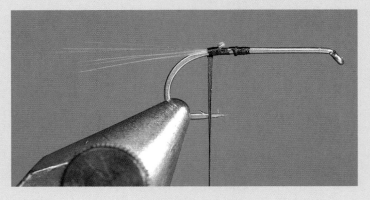

Rubber O-Rings as Hackle and Fur Guards

Rubber O-rings make ideal hackle guards and protect other materials when wrapping the head of the fly. Place the ring on the tube of your bobbin and tie the fly. When you are ready to tie the head, slip the ring onto the fly to hold back the hackle and other materials while wrapping the head.

Durable Tent-Style Wings With Transparent Tape

Cut or burn a featherwing to shape. Next, lay the piece of feather on the sticky side of a piece of Scotch or transparent packaging tape; be sure the side of the feather that forms the outside of the wing is facing up. Apply a very thin coat of cement to the feather, and allow the glue to dry. Finally, clip the tape to match the shape of the featherwing. The end result is a nicely finished tent wing that is ready to tie on the hook and will almost certainly last longer than the rest of the fly. Prepare several to match the wings on grasshoppers, leafcutters, or caddisflies.

Cocking Hackles on Dry Flies

This simple trick seems to make the hackle always wind correctly on the hook. Tie on a dry-fly hackle with the stem parallel to the shank, extending over the eye. Grab the tip of the hackle and pull it over the eye; a small amount of tension puts a small bend in the stem. If you do this correctly, the hackle will stand straight up; if not, pull it a little harder. Finally, grasp and wind the hackle.

Fletch-Dry for Unsinkable Dry Flies

Fletch-Dry is a powder archers use to keep the feathered fletching on their arrows from absorbing water. Fletch-Dry is inexpensive and odorless. Place a small amount of Fletch-Dry in a Ziploc bag. When tying, place the hackles you plan to use in the bag and shake; these feathers will float far longer than untreated hackles. Or place the completed flies in the bag to treat with Fletch-Dry. And don't forget to carry Fletch-Dry in a Ziploc bag in your fishing vest to treat flies when on the water.

Add Tail to a Foam Extended Body

Try this trick to add tails to a foam extended mayfly abdomen. Slightly dull the point of a thin hypodermic syringe needle using fine-grit sandpaper. Next, slowly work the needle through the center of the body and out the back end. Slip two or three Microfibetts through the needle. Hold the Microfibetts the proper length to form the tails of the fly and remove the needle; the tails will remain in place in the body and look very realistic. When you tie the abdomen to the hook, the thread will lock the butt ends of the tails in place.

Snowshoe Dry Flies

The fur from between the toes of a snowshoe hare is crinkled
and traps air bubbles. It is excellent for tying dry flies and emergers.

Tea, Anyone?

The durable paper material in teabags is
an excellent wing material, especially for
mayflies. It is nearly indestructible in water,
takes color well with permanent markers,
and if it has already been steeped, it has
a complete dye job.

High-Floating Indicator Flies

Use closed-cell foam to make a pattern used
as a floating indicator fly; the foam does an
excellent job of supporting a nymph tied
to the dry fly. If the pattern calls for hackle,
make a few extra wraps to give the patterns
additional buoyancy.

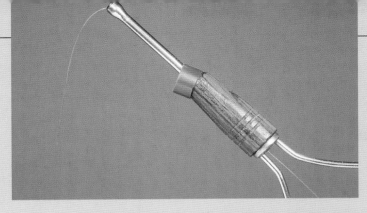

Soda Straw as a Hackle Guard

Do you have problems catching hackle fibers with the thread when completing the head of a fly? Clip a 1/8-inch-wide piece from a wide-diameter soda straw. Slip the narrow plastic guard onto the tube of your bobbin, and tie the fly. When it comes time to wrap the head and whip-finish, pull the piece of straw off the bobbin and onto the front of the fly. Press the straw onto the hackle fibers and tie the head. Whip-finish the thread, clip, and remove the guard.

1 Place a piece of straw on the bobbin and tie the fly.

2 After you wrap the hackle collar, you are ready to tie off the thread.

3 Slip the piece of straw onto the hackle when you're ready to finish the head of the fly. Complete the head.

4 Clip the thread and remove the straw from the hackle. There: a perfect hackle collar.

Add CDC to the Elk-Hair Caddis

All trout anglers use the Elk-Hair Caddis. Add an under-wing of cul de canard to make an Elk-Hair Caddis that floats like a cork. This simple addition is a real improvement to this timeless pattern.

1 Tie the body of the Elk-Hair Caddis.

2 Tie on one or two CDC feathers using three light thread wraps; leave the feathers long for now.

3 Pull the CDC feathers to length. Pull the thread tight, and add one or two more wraps to lock the feathers to the hook.

4 Clip the butt ends of the CDC. Tie on the wing and complete the fly.

Perfecting Parachute Dry Flies

Perfect Parachute Attitude

Put a slight bend in the hook shank about a third of the way down the shank where you plan to tie the parachute wing. Use a pair of needle-nose pliers and slowly bend the hook shank. Tie the wing post and parachute hackle right on top of this bend. The result is a fly that has a perfect attitude on the surface, pushing the hook bend and point below the surface film.

Tiny Parachutes

It's tough to tie a parachute hackle on flies smaller than size 18; the feather gets in the way of the hook eye. The solution is to first tie on the wing and tail of the fly. Next, tie on and wrap the hackle. Tie off the hackle behind the wing, not behind the hook eye. Clip the excess hackle tip, and spin a pinch of dubbing on the thread. Wrap the dubbing on the hook to form the body of the fly; on extra-small flies, there's little reason to tie a distinct abdomen and thorax, so wrap a slender body from the tail to the hook eye. Finally, tie off and clip the thread.

Wrap the Thread and Hackle the Same Direction When Tying a Parachute Dry Fly

Wrapping the thread and hackle in the same direction helps to tighten and lock the feather to the top of the fly. If you wrap the hackle and thread in opposite directions, the thread will actually loosen the feather and weaken the fly.

Wrap a Sturdy Parachute Hackle

Make the wing post, and tie the hackle to the base of the post. When you're ready to wrap the hackle, first place a small drop of Zap-A-Gap Gel on the base of the post. Immediately wrap the hackle on the post. When finished, simply hold the hackle in place for 20 seconds until the glue dries, and clip the excess. The Super Glue Gel holds the hackle and eliminates the frustration of tying off the excess pieces of feather under the parachute collar. Two more methods for wrapping a hackle follow on pages 121–124.

Attaching Yarn Parachute Wing to the Hook

Follow these simple steps to make a wing post using polypropylene or Antron yarn. This method adds no bulk to the fly.

1 Divide the piece of yarn in half; set half of the yarn aside to tie the next fly. Tie on the yarn underneath and perpendicular to the hook shank.

2 Raise the yarn into position. Wrap the thread around the base of the yarn to lock the wing in place. Don't clip the wing to length just yet; continue tying the fly, and cut the wing when you are done.

CHAPTER 5

Better Wet Flies and Nymphs

Embroidery Thread for Wet-Fly Ribs

Embroidery thread, which you'll find in any fabric store, makes great ribbing material for nymphs and wet flies. Embroidery thread is also inexpensive and comes in every imaginable color.

Knotted Tubing for Legs

Place a series of overhand knots in a length of Stretch Tubing to make legs for nymphs. Place the knots about half an inch apart. When tying flies, clip legs as you need them; each leg will have one knotted joint.

Positioning Legs on a Fly

Tying rubber legs on a fly is easy. First, tie on a set of legs parallel to each other using several light wraps of thread. Next, slide the legs into the proper position on each side of the hook. Tighten the thread to lock the legs in place. Continue tying the fly.

This Black & Tan Featherback was tied by the legendary George Grant. Here we see the mottled top of the fly.

Two-Tone Nymph Bodies

Have you ever noticed that most nymphs are darker on top than on the belly? This is easy to replicate on the body of a fly.

First, tie a piece of clear monofilament, D-rib, or similar material to the end of the hook shank. Tie a strip clipped from a feather to the top of the hook; pheasant tail or turkey feathers are perfect for this. Next, wrap the body using some material, such as dubbing, to establish the color of the belly. Finally, pull the strip of feather forward, secure with firm wraps of thread, and then wrap the monofilament to complete an indestructible two-tone abdomen.

Here's the Black & Tan Featherback viewed from the side.

Add Flash to the Dubbing Loop

You can add more than plain fur dubbing to a dubbing loop. Some blended dubbing contains quantities of fine flash material, but you can add your favorite flash to the dubbing loop. Simply cut the flash material short and blend with the dubbing. For collars, add strands of the flash material as long as the hair fibers; simply lay the fibers on top of and parallel to the hair. Insert the material in the loop, spin closed, and wind up the hook shank.

Dry-Fly Hackle for Nymphs

Use dry-fly hackle for making collars on nymphs to create bubbles around the flies in the water and send off trailing bubbles. The stiff fibers resist collapsing like most collar materials such as hen hackle.

Real chironomid have feathery gills. Your imitations should also have this important feature. This fly was tied by the renowned Brian Chan.

Floss for Gills

Real chironomid have small, feathery gills on their heads. Unwaxed dental floss is an ideal material for imitating these small gills.

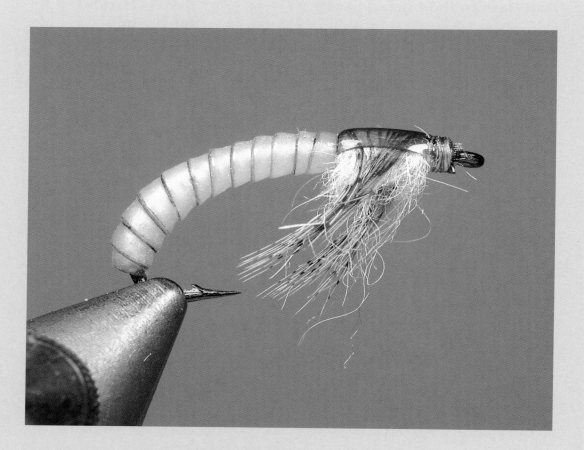

Sili Skin for Realistic Caddisflies

A thin strip of Sili Skin—a common, semi-transparent synthetic material used to make nymph bodies—wrapped over a colored thread base makes super-realistic-looking caddis larvae and pupae. Sili Skin is easy to use and very durable, and the results are satisfying. Your local fly shop carries a whole family of synthetic materials designed for wrapping the bodies on nymphs and caddis larvae. New York's Rob Lewis tied this terrific caddis larva imitation.

Fine-Tuning a Rubber Fly Body

There are a wide variety of materials designed to tie segmented bodies on nymphs and wet flies. With a little practice, you can use these ingredients to make tapered abdomens that have increasingly wider body segments, just like the real insects. Let's see what we can do with a product called Nymph Skin.

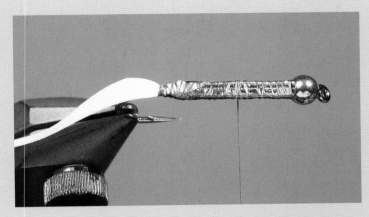

1 Clip the end of the Nymph Skin to a point. Tie the point to the end of the hook shank.

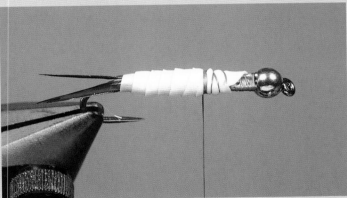

2 Stretch the Nymph Skin. Make one or two wraps of Nymph Skin at the end of the hook to create the tip of the abdomen. Lay a biot on each side of the hook as you wrap the Nymph Skin. Gradually reduce the tension on the material to create a thicker, tapered body.

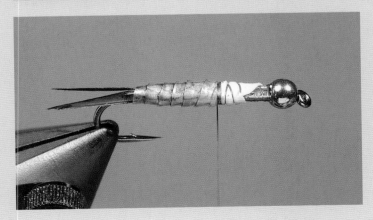

3 Natural-colored Nymph Skin is pretty bland, so color the abdomen using a permanent marker.

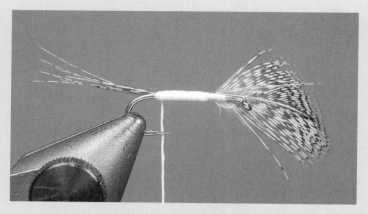

White Thread for Multicolored Bodies

The bodies on some very sparse wet flies are tied using only thread. Use size 3/0 (280 denier) white tying thread to make a realistic-looking multi-colored body.

1 Start the thread on the hook and tie on the tail and wet-fly hackle.

2 Color a length of thread using different perma-nent markers. For instance, color the entire thread with light olive, and then apply narrow bands of brown. Wrap the thread up the hook to form the body. The ink makes a marvelous seg-mented appearance.

3 Wrap the hackle, tie off, and clip the excess. Color the thread with a permanent marker and wrap the head of the fly. Tie off and clip the thread.

Stretch Magic for Better Nymph and Wet-Fly Bodies

Stretch Magic, which is used for making jewelry, makes a good substitute for fly-tying tubing. This material can be purchased at most craft stores. Try wrapping .5-millimeter, clear Stretch Magic over a thread or tinsel body. The Stretch Magic reflects and enhances the color of the underlying material.

Sewing Thread Midge and Wet-Fly Bodies

Sewing and embroidery thread, which comes in dozens of useful colors, is ideal for making the bodies on wet flies and midges. Tie a piece of thread to the end of the hook and twist it tight. Wrap the sewing thread up the hook to create a wonderfully segmented body.

Easy Nymph Gills

Making gills on small nymphs is easy. Tie a piece of ostrich hurl to the hook and spin the herl around the thread. Wrap the herl between the segments of the abdomen. The thread reinforces the herl so it does not break under the strain of fishing, and the wispy herl fibers add lifelike motion to the fly.

Hot Versus Plain Beads

I usually tie ten nymphs at a time; I count out all the materials first and then make the flies. When tying bead-head patterns, I often use plain beads on half of the flies and fluorescent-colored beads on the other half. Later, when fishing low water, I'll start with the drab flies; if the water is high, I'll use the brighter flies with the fluorescent heads.

Dubbing Loops With Fine Thread

Let's say you're tying a small nymph using size 8/0 (70 denier) thread, and you need to make a dubbing loop. Fine thread often breaks when spinning the loop closed. What's the solution? Make a dubbing loop using two or even three strands of thread. This technique greatly increases the strength of the loop and adds little extra bulk to the body of the fly.

Blending in the Dubbing Loop

To make a tail, body, collar, or head of blended colors, stack the colors one on top of the other, insert them into the dubbing loop, and spin it tight. The colors will neatly blend in the loop. If you wish to make a body of banded colors, insert different colors of dubbing next to each other, and then spin the loop closed; wrap the dubbing up the hook to make a multicolored body.

Split Rubber Legs after Tying to the Hook

Some brands of rubber legs come in small bundles with the individual legs fused together. Always leave the legs bound together until tied to the hook. Split them apart with a bodkin after they're tied in place.

A Piece of Tinsel Brightens a Wing Case

Flashback Nymphs and patterns such as the Copper John feature bright wing cases. The theory is that the sparkle simulates the gas generated under the skin of real emerging nymphs. What is clear is that these flies do catch fish. A piece of pearl Mylar tinsel over the wing case, sealed with a drop of epoxy, is an easy way to add this sparkle to your own flies.

In this example, we'll tie the wing case using a strip clipped from a freezer bag. We'll add a piece of Mylar flash to the wing case. This is my version of the Copper John.

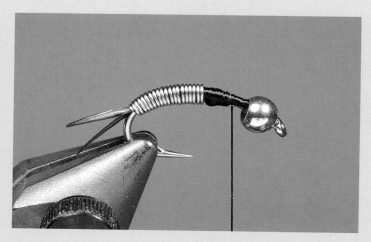

1 Slip the bead on the hook, and tie the biot tail and wire abdomen of the fly.

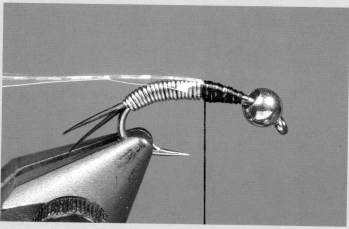

2 Tie on the flash material followed by the clear plastic strip.

3 The thorax on a traditional Copper John is tied using peacock herl, but I am using Hareline Ice Dub, which is a blend of rabbit dubbing with Mylar.

4 Pull the wing case over the top of the fly and tie it off behind the bead.

5 Pull the Mylar over the top of the wing case, tie it off, and clip. Coat the wing case with epoxy. This bright little pattern works well as a single fly or as a dropper in a multi-fly rig.

First Things First?

When making a body with a wire rib, it's common practice to tie on the wire, and then add dubbing to the thread, wrap the body, and wrap the rib. But to save time, spin the dubbing on the thread, and then tie on the wire. When the dubbing reaches the hook, wrap the body. Finally, wrap the wire to form the rib of the fly. This technique eliminates a step and will speed your tying.

Locker-Room Wing Cases

Pre-tape underwrap, which athletes apply before taping their ankles and other joints, is excellent for making nymph wing cases. This 3-inch-wide, open-cell foam comes in rolls from several manufacturers. It usually comes in tan, but other colors are also available. In addition to wing cases, wrap a small strip of material up the hook shank to form a nymph abdomen. A roll costs only about $3 and will last a lifetime.

Sparkly Nymph Backs

Some patterns, such as the Copper John, call for a strip of Mylar tinsel, coated with epoxy, for the wing case. Substitute a piece of Sparkle Braid or a similar material for the plain Mylar. The curved, clear dab of epoxy acts as a sort of lens and gives the Sparkle Braid extra shimmer.

Dyed Pre-Tape Underwrap

You can dye pre-tape underwrap in several useful colors. Buy Rit dye in brown, yellow, or green. Open the box of dye and throw away the directions.

Fill a baby food-sized jar three-quarters of the way with water. (This creates a more concentrated solution than Rit suggests.) Pour the dye into the jar, screw on the cap, and shake it. The dye dissolves instantly. Next, remove the cap and place the jar in a microwave oven set on high for 30 seconds to one minute. Remove the jar from the microwave, and place a piece of foam in the hot dye. Screw the lid back on, and shake the jar for 30 seconds to two minutes. Remove the foam using tweezers (the water will be very hot), and rinse under running water. Squeeze the material in a paper towel and examine the color. If the foam is not dark enough, reheat the dye bath in the microwave and repeat the steps above. If you wish, you can mix dyes—add a little brown to the yellow—to create a custom color. When you are done, dispose of the dye bath. If the jar should break, you could have a disaster on your hands.

Protecting Nymph Bodies from Rotting

There are many brands of latex material designed for making the bodies of nymphs. The problem, however, is that latex rots over time. A simple solution is to tie the body of the fly, and then coat the latex with a material such as Softex or even just head cement or clear fingernail polish. The sealant prevents the latex from deteriorating.

Phil Rowley's dragonfly nymph imitation has a lot of natural swimming action when retrieved through the water.

Better Bulky-Body Swimming Nymphs

Living in Maine, I spend a lot of time fishing trout ponds. In our ponds, as in trout ponds and lakes across North America, dragonflies are a key feature of the trouts' diets. I was always dissatisfied, however, with most of the available dragonfly nymph imitations; they reminded me of more of fat human thumbs, with rubber or hackle-fiber legs attached, than flies. I wanted an easy-to-tie pattern that had good swimming action, and it had to match the large size of a dragonfly nymph. Then I discovered Brian Chan's dragonfly. Brian inserts soft, mottled-colored feather fibers into the tying thread using the split-thread technique, wraps the fibers up the hook, and clips the body to shape. He also adds rubber legs, a wing case, and foam eyes. The entire pattern huffs and puffs when retrieved through the water. I used Brian's pattern as a basis for my own. The only change I made was in the selection of eyes; I substitute extra-small lead dumbbell eyes for the foam, which causes the hook to turn over so the fly sinks quickly and is weedless.

Use this method with marabou or Chickabou feathers to create a wide variety of swimming nymphs that exude fish-enticing action.

Wide-Body Nymphs

While many of our favorite nymph patterns, such as the Hare's-Ear Nymph and Pheasant-Tail Nymph, have bodies that are round in cross-section, the bodies of most real nymphs are slightly flat and broad. This is especially true of mayfly clinging nymphs; they have very thin, broad, wide bodies, so they can easily crawl among the smallest stones on the streambed.

   While a lot of tiers go to great lengths to create broad bodies when tying stonefly nymphs, you can easily make smaller mayfly nymphs with realistically shaped bodies. The simplest method is to tie a piece of lead wire, about equal to the diameter of the hook wire, to each side of the shank. Spiral-wrap the thread up and down the hook to lock the wire to the shank, and then proceed to tie the fly. Use this tip to add weight and create a more realistic-looking fly at the same time.

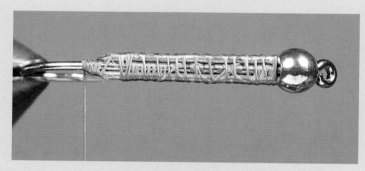

1 I've slipped a bead on the hook and tied a length of wire to each side of the hook. Note that I clipped the ends of the wire near the tail of the fly at angles. This creates a neat transition for wrapping the body material from the hook to the wire base.

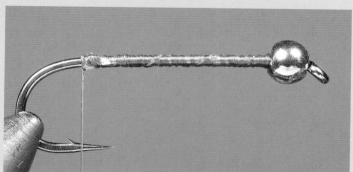

2 Here's the hook-and-wire underbody viewed from the side. The completed fly will be slightly flat and broad, just like a real nymph.

3 Mike Mercer's Poxyback Nymph is typical of a fly tied with a realistically shaped body.

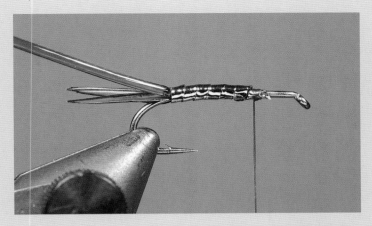

3 Tie the other end of the tubing to the hook. The oil is locked inside the tubing between the thread wraps and the hackle pliers. Wrap a tinsel underbody. Do not remove the hackle pliers.

4 Wrap the tubing up the hook to form the abdomen of the fly. Tie off and clip the excess tubing.

5 Add your choice of abdomen and legs or hackle. I have chosen a thorax of rabbit dubbing and a partridge hackle.

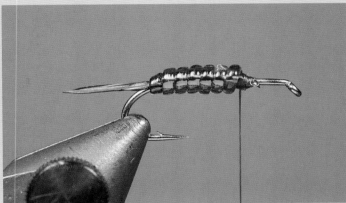

Use a Seam Ripper to Pick Out Dubbing

A seam ripper, which you can purchase at any sewing and most discount stores, is ideal for picking out dubbing when tying Hare's-Ear Nymphs and similar shaggy flies. The pointed tip of the seam ripper picks out the dubbing, and the sharp hook cuts the fibers. A seam ripper is more effective than using a bodkin.

Glue Lead Wire in Place

Before wrapping lead wire or a non-toxic substitute on a hook, put a drop of Super Glue on the hook shank. The glue welds the wire to the hook to create a solid base for the fly; the finished fly will be far less likely to twist on the hook when fishing.

Dubbing Coarseness

There are a variety of natural dubbings. Generally speaking, use coarse angora dubbing for tying large stonefly nymphs, rabbit dubbing for making medium-sized stonefly and mayfly imitations, and squirrel dubbing for tying your smallest nymphs.

Strengthening Featherwings

Spray large tail or wing feathers—such as turkey or goose feathers—with art fixative before clipping small wet-fly wings. The fixative strengthens the feathers and helps prevent the wings from separating while tying.

Hot Spots Catch More Fish

Adding a fluorescent hot spot to a nymph generally makes the fly more productive, especially during off-color water conditions. Magenta, fire orange, fluorescent orange, and fluorescent yellow are all good choices. Many European tiers who specialize in Czech nymphing swear that nymphs and larvae featuring hot spots catch more fish.

Macedonia's Igor Stancev tied this caddis larva imitation with an orange hotspot.

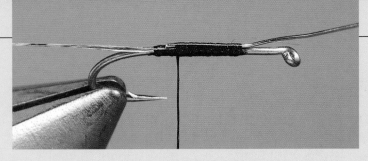

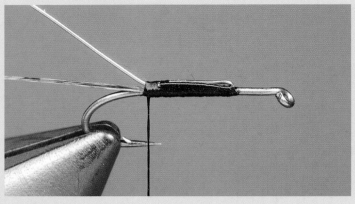

Locking a Rib in a Fly

Almost every beginning tier starts to wrap the wire rib over the body of a fly, only to have the wire break free. The problem is that the tier did not use ample tension or enough thread wraps when tying the wire to the hook. Until you become adept at controlling thread tension, try doubling the tag end of the wire. This technique firmly locks the wire to the hook.

1 Start the thread and tie on the tail of the fly. Tie on a piece of wire. Note that the wire is hanging out over the hook eye.

2 Fold the wire back. Wrap the thread over the doubled piece of wire. This piece of wire is tied fast to the hook and is impossible to pull free.

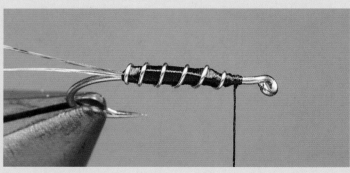

3 Wrap the thread body of the fly. Next, wrap the wire rib. You can complete the fly with a hackle or any abdomen you wish.

4 I added a plain dubbed thorax to this fly. I carry a small platoon of these simple flies to fish as emergers right under the surface of the water. They are extremely effective.

Cul de canard, wrapped as a collar on this Bead-head Sparkle Pupa, mimics the legs and antennae of the real insect.

CDC for Tying Subsurface Flies

European tiers seem well ahead of their North American counterparts when it comes to using cul de canard (CDC) for tying nymphs and wet flies; most Americans and Canadians use CDC only on dry flies. Europeans, however, use CDC to fashion legs, caddis pupa antennae, emerging wing buds, and other parts on flies. The fibers are soft, and they trap air that mimics the gases real nymphs and pupae generate when emerging to the surface.

Hot-Glue Eggs

A hot-glue gun makes some of the best egg flies I've ever seen. The little globs of glue simulate an egg cluster, and the fly readily drops into the strike zone.

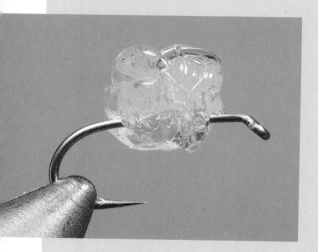

Cover the hook shank with red thread or floss to simulate an eyed egg. Globs of hot glue imitate a small cluster of eggs.

Sparse Wet-Fly Hackle

The most common problem when tying wet flies is using too much hackle. The most effective pattern will have only one wrap of a soft hen or partridge hackle. Remember: The hackle collar represents the legs of an emerging nymph, so you do not want to overdress this feature of the fly.

Scrambled Eggs

Don't forget to add a few egg patterns to your nymph-fishing fly box. When encountering situations when fish are spawning, try fishing an egg pattern along the streambed. Few anglers—except maybe steelheaders and those who visit Alaska—carry eggs, but under the right conditions, these bright little flies work across North America. When trout and land-locked salmon are feeding on real eggs—either their own or another species of fish—an egg imitation is often the only pattern the fish will strike.

Use Zap-A-Gap to Bend Rubber Legs

Here's another method for making permanent joints in rubber legs. Place a drop of Zap-A-Gap on the rubber leg material on the opposite side of the spot where you want the leg to bend. Let the glue set for five to ten seconds. Next, slowly stretch and relax the leg; the leg will set permanently when it recovers. To increase the angle of the bend, simply stretch the rubber over a longer distance. With a little practice, you'll be able to control the amount of bend.

Making Variegated Rubber Legs

You can buy multicolored rubber legs at the fly shop, or you can make your own. Tie the legs to the fly. Twist and hold each leg. Swipe the twisted rubber with a permanent marker. Release the leg to reveal the mottled colored leg. Another option is to place a longer piece of rubber leg material in your vise. Twist and color the entire piece of rubber to make enough to create several sets of multicolored legs.

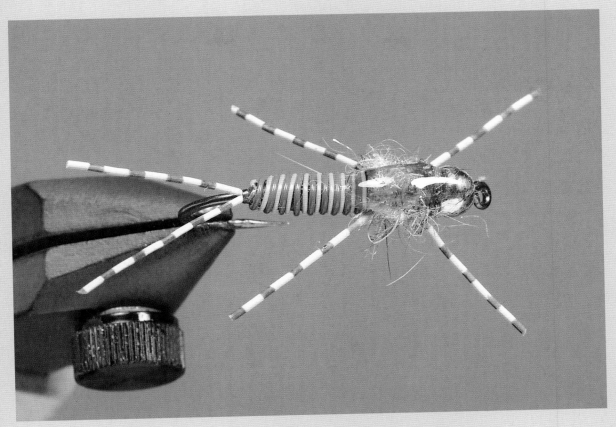

If you like the Copper John, you'll love tying and fishing multicolored, wire-bodied flies.

Two-Tone Wire Flies

Using two strands of different colored wire creates a fantastic segmented appearance on the abdomen of mayfly and stonefly nymphs. Tie the strands next to the base of the tail, and wrap them together to form the abdomen. Large brown and copper wire make a nice golden stonefly imitation. There have been times when these flies caught more trout and landlocked salmon that any other patterns in my fly box.

Deer Hair for Cased-Caddis Larva

Deer hair makes a great case for a caddisfly larva. Really!

Follow these instructions to create a cased caddis imitation that will wow the trout—and your friends. I'm tying the fly using size 3/0 (210 denier) light olive thread. This thread will eventually form the head of the green caddis worm. By the way, I learned this trick from one of my fly-tying heroes, Oliver Edwards. His patterns aren't only brilliant, but they are deceptively easy to tie. This fly is one of my go-to nymph patterns.

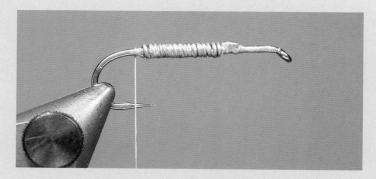

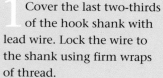
1 Cover the last two-thirds of the hook shank with lead wire. Lock the wire to the shank using firm wraps of thread.

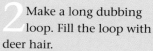
2 Make a long dubbing loop. Fill the loop with deer hair.

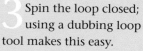
3 Spin the loop closed; using a dubbing loop tool makes this easy.

4 Wrap the spun deer hair two-thirds of the way up the hook. Can you see the caddis case? Not yet? You will in a moment.

5 Clip the deer hair close to the hook shank. Now do you see the outline of our cased caddis larva?

6 Color and rough up the deer-hair case using a brown permanent marker. Take care not to touch the green head of the fly with the marker. You could tie off and clip the thread and fish the fly just as it is, and you would catch trout. But we'll complete this pattern in the next tying tip.

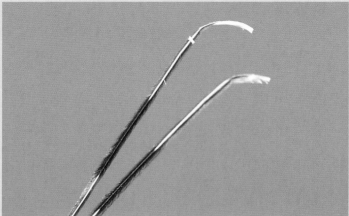

Pheasant-Tail Feathers Make Nice Nymph Legs

Believe it or not, pheasant tail feathers are a great source of material for fashioning realistic nymph and larva legs. Pluck the individual feather fibers down from the thick quill to create neat-looking little jointed feet. Tie the fibers to caddis worms using a loose wrap of thread. Pull the tips of the fibers to adjust the length of the legs. Next, pull the thread tight to cock the fibers out from the body of the fly. Make two more firm wraps of thread, and clip the excess lengths of fiber.

1 Pluck the fibers from the feather in a downward direction.

2 Here are two legs for our cased-caddis larva.

3 Tie a leg onto each side of the fly.

4 Now for the real magic: Color about two inches of thread with a brown marker. Wrap the head of the larva. Tie off and clip the thread. Coat the entire head of the fly with cement. Coat the deer-hair case with fresh head cement. The cement saturates the hair and prohibits it from floating. This unique pattern has become one of my most consistent producers of trout and salmon.

Ostrich Herl Gills for *Hydropsyche* Larva

This is another technique I learned from Oliver Edwards. *Hydropsyche* larvae, which are common to streams around the world, have feathery gills along their bellies. Ostrich herl is perfect for imitating this feature.

Realistic Rubber Nymph Legs

A lot of tiers add rubber legs to their nymphs; a few even take it a step further and add realistic bent joints. Tying knots in all those legs before tying the fly is tedious work. A better solution is to tie on the legs and complete the fly. Next, position the fly in the vise pointing in the direction you'll want the finished bent legs to hang, probably pointing down at about the 5 o'clock position. Lightly touch a leg with a hot-tip cauterizing tool. The heat softens the area, and the leg bends forward. Quickly remove the cauterizing tool. The rubber will cool and return to normal, and you'll have a brilliant-looking jointed leg. You may wish to practice this technique using rubber leg material that has not been tied to a fly. Once you get the hang of the procedure, you'll be ready to tackle the legs on tied flies.

Micro Dumbbells for Tiny Nymphs

Wapsi Fly offers a series of lead eyes that are excellent for adding weight to nymphs. The midget, micro, and mini eyes weigh $1/200$, $1/120$, and $1/80$ ounces, respectively. The micro and mini sizes are small yet heavy enough to turn a hook over (like a Clouser Minnow) to tie imitations of dragonflies and other nymphs that are prone to snag.

A Rifle-Bore Brush Dubbing Rake

A wire rifle-bore brush is perfect for brushing out the dubbing in the thorax of Hare's-Ear Nymphs and similar flies. Fluff out the fibers to simulate the legs of a real nymph.

Tying Rubber Legs on the Fly

Don't waste time carefully positioning the legs on the fly; rubber legs are flexible and easy to use. Just plop the legs onto the top of the hook and make two or three soft thread wraps. Next, pull rubber legs to the sides of the fly, and lock them into position using firm thread wraps.

Biot Tails for Nymphs

Biots are the leading edges of short, durable fibers on the leading edges of turkey and goose wing feathers. Almost all fly shops carry packages of biots dyed in a wide variety of colors. Use individual biots to tie the tails on useful flies such as the Prince Nymph and Copper John. Biots are also perfect for tying the tails on generic stonefly nymphs.

A Tinsel Underbody Brightens the Fly

Whether you use Stretch Tubing, Swannundaze, or some other variety of transparent or semi-transparent material for wrapping the body on your nymphs and wet flies, an underbody of silver or gold tinsel adds a fish-attracting dash of brightness. Fly designer Bill "Bugs" Logan even adds tinsel underbodies to some flies tied with dubbed bodies; although you can't see the tinsel when these flies are dry, they do slightly glow when wet.

Tie a Pregnant Fly

Expert Montana angler and fisheries scientist Andrew Puls reports that research shows trout prefer scud imitations that have orange segments in their bodies. Eggs or parasites cause this orange appearance. Andrew ties his Pregnant Scud with a bright orange glass bead in the body.

When fishing, the small piece of split shot flips the fly over so that the hook point will ride on top. This is a unique pattern, but it does catch fish.

Crawling Cased-Caddis

The next time you're standing in a silted or muddy area of your favorite trout river, take a moment to study the streambed. Do you see shallow, narrow, angular grooves? Those indentations are caused by crawling cased-caddis larvae. If you look further, and the water is clear, there's a good chance you'll actually see one of these insects slowly strolling along the bottom. This is just the sort of display that hooks anglers on aquatic entomology and makes fly fishing such a fascinating pursuit.

In his book, *Oliver Edwards' Flytiers Master-class*, which I highly recommend, Oliver refers to flies designed to match these curious insects. Oliver ties a pattern he calls the Peeping Caddis, and Hans van Klinken makes a fly he calls the Leadhead. Several years ago, while

fishing Italy's Tuscany region for trout and grayling, I saw Hans fish one of his flies along the quietest sections of a river. He retrieved the fly *very* slowly along the bottom, and he caught several nice trout. Under the right circumstances, these flies catch fish!

I suppose you could say that the Peeping Caddis and Leadhead are similar to a Clouser Minnow in that weight is used to turn the hook so the fly rides with the point on top and will not snag the bottom. Rather than a dumbbell, however, Oliver and Hans use a small split shot tied right above the hook eye, and the head of the larva is tied over the bend of the hook. Technically, this configuration causes these flies to move backward (the real larvae crawl with their heads facing forward), but the trout do not mind one bit.

A small piece of singed yarn makes a very convincing caddis larva head. The rubber legs look great, too.

Yarn Head for Cased-Caddis Larva

A singed piece of Antron yarn makes a great head on a cased-caddis larva. Singe the tip of the yarn and tie it to the end of the hook. Add rubber or hackle-fiber legs and tie the case. This example was tied by England's Oliver Edwards.

Mono Leads the Way for Flashabou Rib

A strand of Flashabou, used as a rib, is a good way to add a little sparkle to a nymph. A Flashabou rib, however, is fragile, and can easily break on the rough jaw of a fish. Before tying the Flashabou rib, wrap a rib of 20-pound-test clear monofilament. Next, wrap the Flashabou rib. The monofilament creates a small groove where the Flashabou will lay out of harm's way.

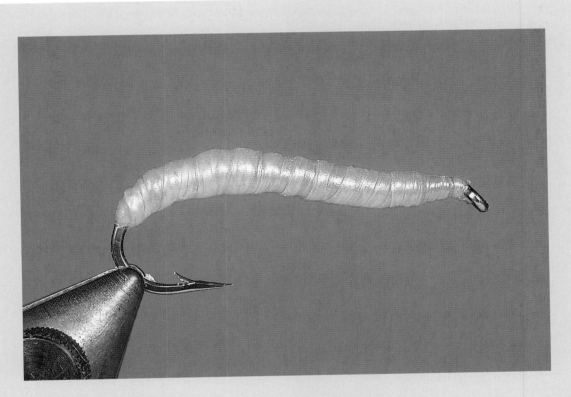

Vladi Condom Worm

The Vladi Condom Worm is becoming an important fly among nymph fishermen. When used as the point fly in a multi-fly rig, it quickly pulls the dropper flies into the strike zone. Use a strip clipped from a non-lubricated latex condom to wrap the worm body. Use a pink marker to color the latex before wrapping the body. Latex will rot over time, so coat the completed fly with Softex or a similar product to seal the body from the air.

Splitting Biot Nymph Tails

When tying a biot nymph tail, such as on a Prince Nymph, place the biots together flaring in opposite directions, and tie them to the end of the hook. Normally the biots will splay in opposite directions, but occasionally they do not. With a bit of preplanning, you can tie perfectly flared tails every time.

First, start the thread on the hook. Leave a 4-inch-long tag of thread hanging off the end of the hook. Next, tie on the biot tails. If the tails splay in opposite directions, similar to the tails on a real nymph, just clip and discard the thread tag. If, however, they do not flair, pull the tag up and forward between the biots. Continue pulling the thread until the tails flair. Finally, tie off the tag, clip the excess, wrap the thread to the base of the tail, and continue tying the fly.

Fuzzy Hackle Fibers as Dubbing

The fuzzy fibers from the base of a hackle make brilliant dubbing for small nymphs and wet flies. They are soft and lifelike in the water and will match the color of the feather. For example, if you use the hackle fiber to tie the tail and legs of the fly, use the fuzzy dubbing to create the thorax or a small head.

Heated Tweezers Shape Nymph Legs

Rubber legs on a nymph look great, but *bent* rubber legs look fantastic. You can knot the legs to create joints prior to tying the flies, but that's a lot of tedious work, and it's often difficult to get the legs to point in the proper direction. Instead, tie the fly with the plain rubber legs in position, and then use a heated, fine-tipped tweezers to bend the joints. Yes, it's possible to overheat the tweezers and melt through a leg, so practice on a plain piece of leg material before working on an actual fly. You will find, however, that this is a very simple technique to learn.

CHAPTER 6

Tips for Tying Big Flies

The Correct Length of Streamer Wings

On streamers and bucktail patterns, keep the wings fairly short. The standard is that the hook should take up two-thirds of the fly, and the wings—extending beyond the end of the hook—constitute no more than one-third of the fly. A streamer tied using this formula swims better and the wings foul less around the hook.

Dense Muddler Heads

Spin the deer hair on the hook, whip-finish the thread, and clip. Next, rough-cut the head to shape. Squirt a small amount of thin head cement into the hair; apply the glue using a bottle with a needle applicator. The glue saturates the hollow deer hair so it does not retain air and sinks. Allow the glue to dry and finish clipping the head. This method creates a very dense deer-hair head suitable for tying sculpin and similar imitations.

Glass Beads for Steelhead Flies

Glass beads have become popular for tying subsurface trout flies, but they are also excellent for creating steelhead patterns. Silver-lined glass beads are especially effective for making the bodies on steelhead flies.

Homemade Eyes for Crustacean Imitations

Nice eyes look cool on a shrimp or crayfish pattern. It's easy to make your own eyes. Here's how:

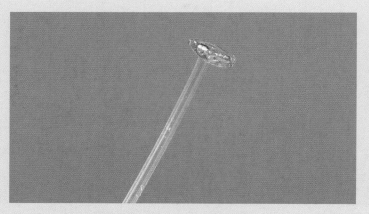

1 Melt the end of a piece of large-diameter monofila-ment: 40- or 50-pound-test is about right. Tamp and flatten the molten mono on the top of your bench.

2 Slip a glass, plastic, or metal bead onto the monofilament. Glue the bead in place using a drop of Super Glue.

3 Tie the two eyes to the hook. The metal beads add both realism and weight to the fly. I added the eyes to the hook on which we tied the monofilament weedguard in a previous tip. This is a good chassis for making a shrimp imitation.

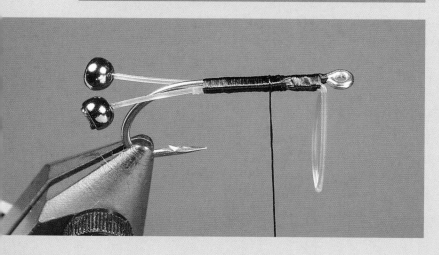

Backing Rod Popper Bodies

Backing rod—the rounded insulation foam used around doors and windows during construction—is a terrific material for making simple popper bodies. Backing rod comes in a couple of very useful diameters, and one package contains enough material to craft hundreds of poppers. Look for backing rod in the insulation department of your local home-improvement store.

Colored Weedguards

On a saltwater fly, color bands on the weedguard to match the color scheme of the body. Black, olive, and similar permanent makers are perfect for this purpose. Coloring the weedguard makes it look like an integral part of the pattern.

Save Thick Cement for Special Uses

Don't discard thickened head cement. Use thick head cement to glue together the feathers used in the tails and wings of streamers.

Worm Hooks for Weedless Flies

Rather than using weedguards or bendback hooks, try worm hooks—the type used by conventional-tackle bass anglers—for making weedless flies. Flies tied on worm hooks are often superior at hooking fish and preventing snags; plus they allow you to tie many unique patterns. Try using the long-neck VMC 6319BN; this hook has extra room between the hook eye and bend for tying.

Improved Looped Weedguard

Before tying on a looped monofilament weedguard, bend the mono in half and pinch a V in the loop using pliers. Next, bend the legs of the weedguard 90 degrees. Now you can easily tie the feet in the legs to the hook and create a perfect weedguard.

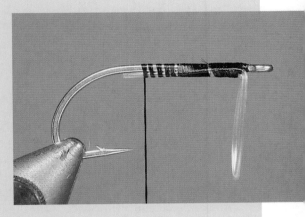

Take a moment to prepare the weedguard before tying it to the fly.

Debarb Before Tying the Fly

Do you wish to tie a fly on a barbless hook? Then mash down the barb before making the fly. Place the debarbed hook in the vise, and lightly flex it up and down to make sure that it doesn't snap. There's nothing more frustrating that taking the time to tie a nice fly only to have the hook break because debarbing weakened the hook wire.

Permanent Markers on the Go

Who says you have to color all of your flies at the bench? Carry a selection of markers with you when you fish. Store the markers in a Ziploc bag to keep them fresh. Now you can color a fly to match the conditions. For example, tie crab imitations in cream, and later color them brown or green to match the local crabs.

Carry your favorite markers with you, and fine-tune the colors of your flies when you fish.

Micro Suede as a Body Material

Micro Suede is great for imitating a minnow body, and the material is inexpensive and comes in many colors. You can purchase Micro Suede by the yard and split it with friends. To use, simply cut a minnow shape, tie it to the hook, add a foam head, and you have a lifelike baitfish imitation that really catches fish. You can also use Micro Suede to make crab legs, crayfish pincers, and thin lifelike San Juan worms.

Taming Splayed Hackle Wings

When tying patterns with splayed hackle wings, such as Deceivers and Seaducers, it's sometimes difficult to keep the feathers properly aligned; the hackles often spin into undesirable angles. There is a simple solution to this problem. Strip the fibers from the bases of the hackles until the feathers are the desired length. Next, align the hackles so that they curve out, and place a drop of cement at the base of the wing. Hold the feathers until the glue thickens, and then set the wing aside to dry. When tying the fly, you'll apply the wing as a bunch of feathers and maintain better control.

A Fly that Both Sinks and Floats

Try tying a fly with both weight to make it sink and foam to make it float. Does this make sense? You bet it does.

Tie on heavy dumbbell eyes behind the hook eye to cause the nose of the fly to sink, and add a piece of closed-cell foam to make the rear of the fly float upward. Try gluing a thin piece of foam on the hide side of a piece of rabbit strip, or use foam as the carapace of a shrimp fly. Such a pattern is great for bouncing along the bottom; it has a more natural posture than a typical fly that lays flat on the bottom. This sort of pattern also has an exaggerated jigging action when you strip the fly through the water.

Best Bucktail for Hair-Wing Streamers

For tying wings on streamers, select bucktail with the straight-est possible hair, like that on this classic Micky Finn. Cork-screwed hair makes thick, bulkier wings, which might be fine for making some saltwater patterns, but is poor for making smaller saltwater streamers. Visit your local fly shop when purchasing bucktails; this is one material you should see before buying. Examine all the bucktails in the colors you need, and consider only those with fine, long, straight hair.

Foul-Free Rabbit-Strip Tails

Using a length of monofilament is another way to prevent a rabbit-strip tail from fouling around the hook when fishing.

1 Melt a small ball on the end of the mono. Thread the straight end of the mono through a small hole in the strip.

2 Tie the end of the monofilament to the hook.

3 Tie the end of the bunny strip to the hook. The mono prevents the tail from fouling around the hook, but the fur and tip of the tail retain their great swimming action.

Bead Tail a Shrimp Pattern

Beads strung on a piece of fluorocarbon make a nice tail on a shrimp imitation. Tie your favorite shrimp body, and then tie a piece of 12-pound-test fluorocarbon to the hook eye. Slide four or five colored beads onto the fluorocarbon. Add a small metal bead, grasp the fluorocarbon with hackle pliers, and thread the fluorocarbon back through the beads. Adjust the fluorocarbon until a quarter-inch-wide loop is sticking out of the metal bead and there are small gaps between the plastic beads. Crimp the metal bead to trap the loop of fluorocarbon. Finally, tie the loose end of the fluorocarbon to the hook eye. When fishing, tie your leader to the loop and cast the fly. As you strip the shrimp through the water, the tail and body will move in a very convincing manner, and the beads rattle and give off fish-attracting vibrations in the water.

Bottle Cap Crab Bodies

The pull-off caps from plastic milk and juice cartons make excellent crab bodies. They are easy to trim to shape and have neutral buoyancy. After gluing on legs, eyes, and pincers, fill the belly with a material to make the crab float on the surface, hover in the water column, or sink.

To make the crab float, use a small amount of white Gorilla Glue mixed with an equal amount of water. Thoroughly mix the water and glue, and fill the cavity. Fill the cap with Sparkle Body to make the fly hover in the water column, or add split shot to the Sparkle Body to make the crab sink. Color the plastic cap with paint to match the crabs in your local waters.

Easier Hook Sharpening

Many saltwater anglers are fanatics about sharpening hooks; they even sharpen new hooks before tying their flies. A fly-tying vise is a good aid to hook sharpening. Place the hook in the vise, and then sharpen the point. The vise holds the hook firmly and makes it much easier to sharpen the hook.

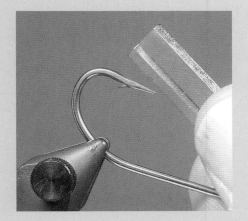

Mount the hook in the vise and sharpen the hook.

Tail Facing Up or Down?

Most leech and bunny patterns are tied with the leather side of the tail facing down, but consider this: most fish see these flies looking up. When making a fly featuring a tail with a rabbit Zonker strip, tie the rabbit strip on with the fur side facing down so the fish easily see all that waving, pulsating fur.

Locking in a Heavy Tail

If you're wrapping over the butt ends of a marabou tail to build an underbody for a bulkier fly, the butt ends (or any soft material) will have a tendency to roll around the hook as you wrap forward. You also do not want to clip the butt ends short or you will create a hump in the completed body. The solution? After securing the tail, lift the butt ends of the marabou and wrap the thread forward to the beginning of the underbody. Next, pull the butts forward, tie them to the hook, clip the excess, and spiral-wrap the thread back over the underbody. This locks the marabou butt ends in place to create a thick underbody.

1 Don't clip the butt ends short, like on this fly. That bump at the base of the tail will create an unsightly bump in the completed body.

2 Instead, use the butt ends of the tail material to create a level underbody. Use this technique when tying with marabou, bucktail, and similar thick materials.

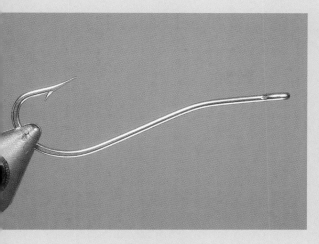

Snag-Free Flies for Shallow-Water Fish

Small flies are favored for catching bonefish and other skittish, skinny-water fish. You want these flies to ride with the hook points on top so they do not snag the bottom. Instead of tying weights—bead chain or small dumbbells—to the tops of the hooks so they flip over while fishing, slightly bend the hooks to create small keels. This shape of hook is used to tie the famous Bend-Back saltwater fly, and it is a great way to create smaller flies that flip over, are less likely to snag, and are light enough to enter the water with minimal splash.

Place a slight bend in the hook shank to create a Bend-Back hook.

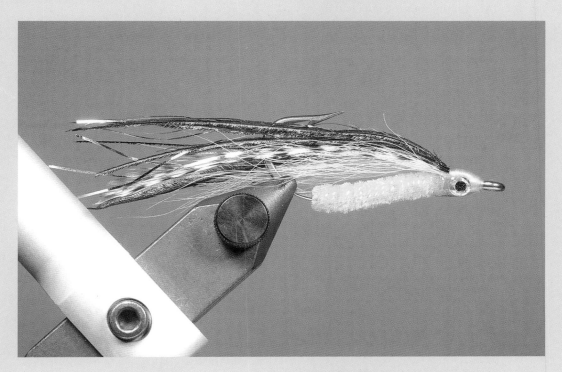

A classic Bend-Back will not snag the bottom when you fish shallow-water flats.

Filling the Gap on a Popper

Wall Spackle is ideal for filling the hook gap on a popper body prior to painting. Allow the Spackle to dry, and easily sand to shape.

Tying Bucktail on a Clouser Minnow

Sometimes it's difficult to tie the bucktail on a Clouser Minnow; the bucktail has a tendency to flair, and many tiers resort to pulling out unruly hairs. A better method than removing hairs is to grab the clump of bucktail by the butt ends with one hand, and use the thumb and forefinger of the other hand to rub and twist the hair together by rubbing from the butt end up to the tips. This simple technique sort of weaves the bucktail together, thus preventing flaring and making it easy to lay on the hook shank.

Stronger Poppers and Crease Flies

When gluing a foam popper head or Crease Fly body to a hook shank, it is always best to first wrap a good layer of thread along the entire length of the hook shank. The thread reduces the tendency of the foam to roll around the hook when building the body of the fly. It also allows the glue to adhere to and penetrate the thread, which is better than the steel shank of the hook.

Taming Wood Duck and Teal Feathers

When using wood-duck and teal flank feathers, cut usable strips from a pair of matching feathers. Leave some of the quills attached to help control the feather fibers when mounting the strips to the hook.

Perfectly Placed Wings

It's easy to tie wings on the top of a streamer or wet fly. Hold the wings over the top of the hook. Wrap the thread over the top of the wings. Next, start another wrap. Pull the thread straight up, and lower the wings to the hook. Do not release the wings, and complete the second wrap. Tighten the thread, and examine the wings to check that they are on top of the hook. Wiggle the wings into position if necessary; it won't take much effort to get them into place. Make a couple more firm wraps of thread to lock the wings to the fly. This technique prevents the wings from rolling around the hook.

Finishing Saltwater Flies

Tying a whip-finish seems like a trivial issue, but for saltwater flies it's important.

Heads on saltwater patterns are often larger than on freshwater flies, and they require many more turns of thread to complete the profiles. You don't want the thread windings to collapse and slip down the tapered head during the finishing operation. Start the whip-finish near the eye of the hook and wrap up the taper. Once you release the tool, the coils of thread tighten and do not slip down the head.

Scales on Poppers

Adding fish scales to poppers is easy. First, paint the popper body any color you desire. Next, fold a small piece of window screen around the body. Spray the body and screen with the next color of your choice. When you remove the screen, the body will have a nice, fish-scale appearance.

Improved Anti-Fouling Loop for Tails

A lot of tiers add monofilament anti-fouling loops beneath the tails of flies to prevent the materials from fouling around the hooks. But what should you tie on first: the loop or the tail? Most tiers tie the loop to the hook and then add the long tail; that seems more natural. Other tiers, however, say it's better to add the loop after tying on the tail. First, tie the tail to the hook. Next, bend a piece of 15- or 20-pound monofilament into a loop. Slip the loop under the tail into position; the ends of the mono should extend beyond the base of the tail. Tie the ends of the mono to the top—not the sides—of the hook. The loop slightly encircles the base of the tail and does a better job of preventing fouling.

1 Tie on the tail of the fly; in this case, an orange bunny strip.

2 Slip a loop of monofilament under the tail. Tie the ends of the loop to the top of the hook. The loop slightly raises the tail away from the hook.

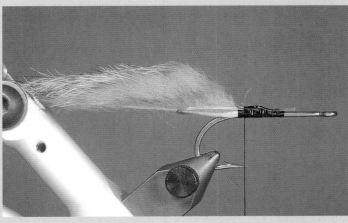

Afraid of spooking fish on the flats? Then tie at least a few flies on flat-finished hooks.

Flat-Finished Hooks for Clear-Water Flats

Use flat-finished hooks for tying flies to fish clear-water flats for bonefish, stripers, and permit; redfish and drum often inhabit off-color water, where the flat finish is not so important. The shiny flash that radiates off the hook bend and point in bright conditions spooks as many fish as anything else in the game. Flat-finished hooks, such as the Tiemco TMC811S, are less bright and spook fewer wary fish.

Trimming Muddler Heads

A Muddler Minnow has a trimmed deer-hair head and nicely shaped collar. When completing the fly, the goal is to clip the head—not the collar! Unfortunately, this task is not as easy as it sounds. Use a piece of Scotch tape to protect the collar while trimming the deer-hair head.

Fold tags on both ends of the tape, and remove some of the adhesive on the leg of your pants. Next, fold back the deer-hair collar of the fly. Snuggly wrap the tape around the collar. Clip the head to shape with a razor or scissors; the tool will glance right over the tape. When you're done trimming, pull the tape off the fly.

Scratch the Hook Before Tying on a Dumbbell

Tom Schmuecker owns Wapsi Fly in Moutain Home, Arkansas. Wapsi was the first company to distribute lead dumbbell eyes and today sells hundreds of thousands of dumbbells each year. Tom advises to scratch the hook with a file before tying on the dumbbell. The scratches, Tom says, give the thread something to bite into and help secure the dumbbell in place.

Guide Tying Tip

Florida's Capt. John Kumiski, who is both an expert angler and tier, says: "I avoid using feathers whenever possible. They are the most difficult and time-consuming materials to use. Good substitutes include rabbit strips, arctic fox or Finnish raccoon hair, as well as a variety of synthetic materials. I need to tie a lot of flies—fast—and don't have time to mess around with getting feathers to lay on correctly. These other materials are easier to use, and they probably have better action in the water, too."

Cover the Rough Ends of Hooks

Capt. Ray Stackelek, one of Rhode Island's leading saltwater guides, points out that the end of the wire used to form the eyes of some stainless steel hooks often has a small, sharp barb that can fray leaders. Captain Stackelek recommends wrapping the thread on the base of these hook eyes when finishing the heads of flies. This covers any tiny barbs and protects leaders from damage, and it might prevent losing fish.

Cover the end of the hook wire with thread wraps to protect the tippet from microscopic barbs.

The head on this pattern enhances the baitfish profile of the fly.

EZ-Body Head on a Fly

Want to tie a realistic-looking streamer? Then include a head of EZ-Body Tubing. In addition to imitating the shape of a baitfish, the tubing is an ideal place to affix adhesive eyes. Cut a short section of tubing and slip it over the hook and tie down. You'll have to clip and then restart your tying thread to accommodate the tubing, but that's small effort for such satisfying results.

Flats Flies for Various Depths

For catching bonefish, red-fish, permit, and other flats species, your fly box should contain the same patterns tied in different weights to fish various depths. Use different sizes of dumbbells, and add a few flies tied with bead-chain eyes. Be prepared with flies to fish water from a few inches to a few feet deep.

Proper Dumbbell Spacing for a Clouser Minnow

Leave plenty of room between the hook eye and dumbbell eyes when tying a Clouser Minnow, probably more room than you think you'll need to complete the head of the fly. On the original pattern, the dumbbell was tied almost halfway down the hook shank!

Baitfish Are Not Swimming Paintbrushes

There is no rule saying the ends of the materials used to tie the wing on a streamer must be even like a paintbrush. In fact, this fly will look less realistic in the water than one tied with the materials—bucktail, synthetic hair, and flash—staggered. When making the wing, stagger small bunches of material to create a more natural silhouette. Another method is to grab the entire wing in one hand, and with the other hand slowly pull pieces from the middle of the wing to stagger the ends. Tie the entire bunch of materials to the hook to form the wing of the fly.

This is a very simple yet effective shrimp imitation. It has all the features that suggest this important form of saltwater forage.

Thin Skin for Shrimp Back

This remarkably simple shrimp imitation features a carapace tied using a strip of clear Thin Skin. Thin Skin also comes in orange (which would work equally well on this fly) and tan for making tan-colored shrimps.

Tee It Up

Insert a golf tee into the mouth of a Crease Fly. The top of the tee makes a nice cupped mouth in the face of the fly.

Add Eye Appeal to the Heads of Your Flies

After finishing the head of a fly using black thread, add a narrow band of another color thread (white, red, or yellow) to add a little eye appeal to the pattern. Carrie Stevens used this trick to tie the Gray Ghost and her other famous streamers, and you can, too.

Tying a Dense Muddler Minnow Head

Instead of spinning deer hair to make the head on a Muddler Minnow, stack two bunches of hair, one on top of another. Tie one bunch on the bottom of the hook using very firm thread wraps. Maintain thread pressure, and tie a second bunch on top of the hook opposite the first bunch of hair. Tighten the thread very firmly to flair the hair. The result will be a dense Muddler head with a very full collar.

Tips for Dressing Classic Salmon Flies

Underwing Substitute Feathers

The underwings on classic salmon flies are usually white-tipped brown turkey, golden pheasant tippet, or pheasant body feathers. Hackle of all colors and textures is a splendid substitute. Think of adding a strand or two of Flashabou or Krystal Flash if you plan to fish with the fly.

Substitute for Silk Floss

Silk floss is available for tying flies, but it is expensive. While it might be mandatory for tying flies destined for mounting behind glass, it's not necessary for tying flies for fishing. Dacron floss is easy to handle, comes in myriad colors, looks great on a finished fly, and holds its color when wet. Also, silk thread and floss are natural materials and have a tendency to deteriorate over time; Dacron does not.

Interesting Veil Feathers

There are hundreds of interesting tiny feathers other than expensive chatterer, toucan, and Indian crow. Pheasant, quail, grouse, woodcock, and numerous other game birds are loaded with beautifully mottled feathers that are perfect for tying veils and cheeks on streamers.

Mounting Shoulders and Cheeks

If the feathers used to create the shoulders or cheeks on a fly flair out under thread pressure, try shaping the quills so the feathers curve in against the sides of the fly. Lightly draw the inside of the quill over scissors or a fingernail, similar to curling ribbon.

Managing Unruly Feathers

Some feathers have a nasty habit of turning and rolling around the hook under thread pressure. Pheasant crest feathers, which are used as tails and toppings on many classic streamers and salmon flies, are good examples of feathers that won't sit still. The best solution is to flatten the base of the quill using a smooth-jawed needle-nose pliers. This flat platform is far less likely to twist and turn on the hook. If you continue to encounter problems, tie the flattened quill to the fly using two or three light wraps of thread and then place a drop of Super Glue on the thread. Make two more wraps and allow the glue to dry. The glue welds the feather to the hook in the correct position, and you may continue tying the fly.

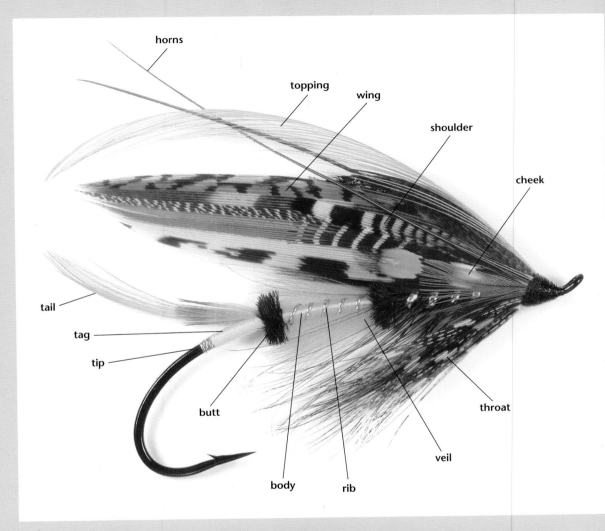

horns

topping

wing

shoulder

cheek

tail

tag

tip

butt

body

rib

veil

throat

Dick Talleur tied this handsome Jock Scott. It contains almost all the parts of a classic Atlantic salmon fly.

Tips for Dressing Classic Salmon Flies

Protect a Black Hook With a Piece of Cardboard

The black japanned finish on a salmon hook will scratch on the metal vise jaws. Fold a tiny piece of thin cardboard around the hook and then place the hook in the vise. The cardboard protects the hook from scratching.

Veils on a Salmon Fly Wing

Bronze mallard is a difficult feather to use. Try this old method from the United Kingdom to put mallard veils on the wing of a classic salmon fly. Cut a section of mallard from a matching set of feathers, leaving the quills attached. Lay one section directly on top of the other, holding them firmly at the quills. Stroke the feathers toward the tips until they come together in a fairly straight line. Cut the sections from the quills. Center the strips of mallard on top of the married wing, which is already tied on the fly, and adjust the mallard for proper length. Fold the strips down so that 50 percent of the mallard lies on each side of the married wing. Finally, tie the strips in place. This is a foolproof method for getting bronze mallard to sit correctly on a classic salmon pattern.

Tying on Horns

Horns, which are usually made from macaw fibers, are the final touch on many classic salmon flies. Lightly tie a fiber onto each side of the head of the fly; the horns should slant back along the sides of the wing. If the horns are not perfectly placed, you can easily retie them until you are pleased with the appearance of the fly. Lock the horns in place using two or three firm wraps of thread.

How Many Wraps in a Tinsel Rib?

Do you know the answer? Most authorities agree that the rib on a classic salmon fly, or streamer tied on a regular-length streamer hook, should have five evenly spaced wraps of tinsel.

Taming Golden Pheasant-Crest Feathers

Golden pheasant-crest feathers, sometimes called toppings, are a key component of many classic patterns. These feathers, however, are usually slightly crooked and lack nice curvature. Straightening and curving a pheasant crest feather is simple.

First, soak the feather in water. Next, place the feather on a glass. Select a glass with the circumference that matches the desired curve of the finished feather; a brandy snifter is ideal because the tapered glass offers a wide range of circumferences. Carefully place the quill feather around the glass. Allow the feather to completely dry. When dry, the feather will assume the curvature of the glass.

1 Soak the topping in water. Next, place the feather on a glass. Allow the topping to dry.

2 Remove the feather from the glass. This topping has a perfect curved shape.

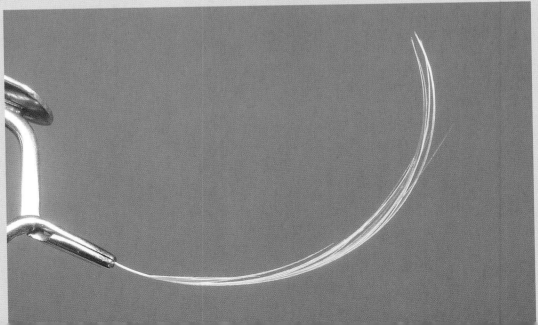

Repairing Jungle Cock Eyes

Jungle cock feathers are expensive, but sometimes you can get a bargain on less-than-prime feathers. These feathers are perfectly acceptable for tying flies for fishing.

The most common problem is that the hard feathers crack; these are called split feathers. Repairing split jungle cock feathers is simple. First, coat the back of a split feather with thick head cement. Grasp the base of feather with one hand, and draw the feather between the thumb and forefinger of the other hand. Repeat, drawing the feather between your fingers until the split is repaired, and allow the cement to dry. Apply another drop of cement to strengthen the repair.

1 Here's a split jungle cock feather. We can easily repair it and use it to tie a fly.

2 Place a drop of cement on the back of the feather. Draw the feather between your thumb and forefinger several times until the glue dries.

3 Our repaired jungle cock nail feather looks almost like new.

Monofilament Thread over Adhesive Eyes

Use mono thread over adhesive eyes to shape the eyes to the head. Coat the head with epoxy.

You can't see it, but I placed a couple of wraps of clear monofilament thread over the eyes of this fly before coating the head with epoxy.

Tying Off Monofilament Thread

Fine monofilament thread is great for tying streamers and saltwater flies, but it is slippery and difficult to tie off. Always tie off monofilament thread using two whip-finishes, and coat the knots with head cement.

How Many Ostrich Herl Wraps

The fibers of an ostrich herl butt should sweep toward the rear of the fly. Six wraps are usually enough to create a dense, attractive herl butt on a classic streamer.

Monofilament or Gel-Spun Thread for Slender Thunder Creek Bodies

Keith Fulsher rocked the fly-fishing world in the early 1970s with the introduction of his Thunder Creek series of streamers. Keith argued that match the hatch goes beyond tying flies that imitate insects; he created a series of new patterns that match common baitfish. Use monofilament thread to tie ultra-thin bodies on Thunder Creek streamers; the monofilament compresses the butt ends of the deer hair more than other types of thread and makes small heads. You'll get the same effect if you substitute gel-spun thread.

Primping Synthetic Hairs

Synthetic hairs such as Polar Fiber and Craft Fur are great for making the wing of a streamer, but you should take a moment to prepare the material before tying it to the hook. First, select a bunch of hair. Next, divide, stack, and restack the hair between your fingers to create the perfect profile of a small baitfish that tapers toward the rear of the fly. These procedures take just a few seconds, but the result will improve the appearance of your flies.

Fish Skulls for Better Streamers

A new product called Fish Skulls is popping up in fly shops. These oblong weights, manufactured by Flymen Fishing Company, won a Dealer's Choice Award at the 2010 International Fly Tackle Dealer show. They are very easy to use: tie the fly, coat the thread head with Super Glue, and slip the Fish Skull into place. Restart the thread between the hook eye and nose of the skull, and make a few wraps to lock the skull into place. Fish Skulls come in a variety of sizes and colors.

Spacing Splayed-Feather Tails

When tying splayed feathers on a fly, like the tail on a tarpon pattern, it is often helpful to tie in a trimmed hackle as a spacer. Tie this hackle firmly on top of the hook. Next, tie on the splayed feathers; one, two, or three feathers for each half of the tail. Lock the tail to the hook using firm thread wraps. When you are pleased with the appearance of the tail, lift the spacing hackle and clip it tight against the hook. The spacing feather keeps the tail feathers from rolling around the hook while you tie the fly.

Stronger Monofilament Attachment Points

There are many ways to attach monofilament weedguards and mono joints to articulated, jointed flies; most are time-consuming and create excessive bulk on the hook shank. Crimping the ends of the monofilament using toothed pliers, and then simply tying the mono to the hook shank, simplifies the process. The small grooves created by the pliers give the thread something to bite into. This decreases the amount of thread wraps you'll need to secure the monofilament to the hook. By crimping the mono, you are increasing its surface area and creating small grooves that the tying thread can bite into. It's a lot like adding chains to your tires in the winter.

Proper Popper Underbody

Wrap the hook shank with yarn or chenille before gluing a popper body to the hook. This underbody strengthens the glue bond between the hook and the popper.

Index

poppers, 95, 159, 166
punch cutters, 89
wings, 97
Foil, 32, 89
Fur, 110
beaver, 58
fox, 169
mink, 58
muskrat, 58
rabbit/hare, 38, 51, 57, 116, 141, 143, 162, 163, 169
synthetic, 71
woodchuck underfur dubbing, 46

Gills, 127, 131, 151
Gloves, surgical, 137
Glue, 37, 45, 51, 55, 59, 108, 119, 143, 158, 163, 172, 178
See also specific products; Cement; Epoxy
bottle as paint applicator, 88
bottle station, 77
clearing a tube, 42
finishing thread head with, 26
instead of head cement, 62
Glue gun, hot, 146
Golf tee, 171
Gorilla Glue, 163
Grasshoppers, 108
Gray Ghost, 11, 171
Gudebrod, 66

Hackle, 101, 103, 116, 127, 130, 146, 172
See also Feathers; Quills
changing the curve in a, 29
cocking, 115
collar, extra-thick dry-fly, 100, 102, 108
fuzzy fibers, 156
grizzly, 106
heating, 107
hen, 19, 127, 146
parachute, 119, 121-123
partridge, 141, 146
reconditioning old capes, 45
repairing bent, 99
saddle, 21, 39, 102
splayed, 160
storing, 42, 52
sweet spot of, 109
Hackle gauge, 81
Hackle guard, 115, 117
Hacksaw blade, 94

Hair, 95, 101, 112
antelope, 60
calftail, 36, 37, 42, 46, 108
deer, 60, 61, 76, 88, 91, 92, 94, 99, 148-150, 157, 161, 164, 166, 169-171, 177
elk, 106
flaring, best for, 61
polar bear, 46
raccoon, 46, 169
spinning, best for, 61
squirrel, 32, 37, 42, 55, 143
steaming, 61
synthetic, 71, 92, 170, 177
trimming, 61, 76, 88
Hair clippers, electric, 91
Hair combs, 24, 92
Hair conditioner, 45
Hair packer, 92
Hair scrunchies, 76
Hair stacker, 5, 27, 32, 36, 46, 60, 70
cleaning, 73
lipstick tube, 95
wooden, 85
Hair straightening iron, 76
Half-and-Half, 3
Half-hitch knots, 4, 40, 60, 83
Hammer, 32
Hands, washing, 1
Hareline Dubbin
Hare's Wiggle, 138
Ice Dub, 133
Hare's-Ear Nymph, 14, 94, 136, 142, 151
Head of fly, 45, 49, 117
See also Eyes
finishing, 45, 171
Hex patterns, 57, 111
Hook(s), 26, 27, 51, 119, 120, 126, 127, 129, 131, 134, 135, 137, 143, 148-149, 153, 154, 156, 157, 162, 164, 166, 167, 170-172, 178
barbless, 27, 159
bending, 165
covering rough ends of, 169
dubbing loop over, 33, 91
flat-finished, 168
hackle size and, 106
magnet for holding/retrieving, 69, 81
offset, 35
sharpening, 163
in vise, 78, 80, 163, 174
worm, 159